ROMULUS PUBLIC LIBRARY
11121 Wayne Road
Romulus, MI 48174
1 (734) 942-7589

W9-AUD-990

YA 613.8
Bes

9/14

IT HAPPENED TO ME

Series Editor: Arlene Hirschfelder

Books in the It Happened to Me series are designed for inquisitive teens digging for answers about certain illnesses, social issues, or lifestyle interests. Whether you are deep into your teen years or just entering them, these books are gold mines of up-to-date information, riveting teen views, and great visuals to help you figure out stuff. Besides special boxes highlighting singular facts, each book is enhanced with the latest reading lists, websites, and an index. Perfect for browsing, there are loads of expert information by acclaimed writers to help parents, guardians, and librarians understand teen illness, tough situations, and lifestyle choices.

SUBSTANCE ABUSE

THE ULTIMATE TEEN GUIDE

SHERI MABRY BESTOR

IT HAPPENED TO ME, NO. 36

THE SCARECROW PRESS, INC.
Lanham • Toronto • Plymouth, UK
2013

Published by Scarecrow Press, Inc.
A wholly owned subsidiary of The Rowman & Littlefield Publishing Group, Inc.
4501 Forbes Boulevard, Suite 200, Lanham, Maryland 20706
www.rowman.com

10 Thornbury Road, Plymouth PL6 7PP, United Kingdom

Copyright © 2013 by Scarecrow Press, Inc.

All rights reserved. No part of this book may be reproduced in any form or by any electronic or mechanical means, including information storage and retrieval systems, without written permission from the publisher, except by a reviewer who may quote passages in a review.

British Library Cataloguing in Publication Information Available

Library of Congress Cataloging-in-Publication Data

Bestor, Sheri L. M.
  Substance abuse : the ultimate teen guide / Sheri Mabry Bestor.
    pages cm. — (It happened to me ; No. 36)
  Includes bibliographical references and index.
  ISBN 978-0-8108-8558-5 (cloth : alk. paper) — ISBN 978-0-8108-8559-2 (ebook)
  1. Substance abuse—Juvenile literature. 2. Teenagers—Substance use—Juvenile literature. I. Title.
  HV4999.Y68B47 2013
  613.8—dc23
                                                          2013011091

∞™ The paper used in this publication meets the minimum requirements of American National Standard for Information Sciences—Permanence of Paper for Printed Library Materials, ANSI/NISO Z39.48-1992. Printed in the United States of America

3 9082 12683 1372

For You, who went through this, and for Those, too, who went through this with you.
For Whitnie, Kaiti, and Hailie . . . three teenagers whose brilliant light I see clearly.
Namaste.

Contents

Disclaimer

While one of the intentions I had for writing this book was to help people understand substance abuse disorders to then move toward abolishing the stigma associated, still, at the time of the book's first printing, judgment continued to surround those who are associated with this disease.

For this reason, many of the contributors in this book have chosen to change their name or other slight details to protect themselves and their families with privacy. Though slight details may have changed, their stories remain the same. Their truth is what I want you to read.

The topic of substance abuse, like most researched topics, continually presents new and updated theories and data. That said, I ask you to consider the concepts of the book and the value they may have in giving you new insights and new perspectives. By the time you are reading these words, some of the statistics in this book will already be outdated. The reasons behind providing the data, however, remain.

Thank you.

Note from the Author

"If we wonder often, the gift of knowledge will come."—Arapaho

While I was writing this book, when people would find out what the title was, a typical question they would ask me was, "Why did you choose *this* topic?"

It was a fair enough question, and my answers were pretty much the same:

"I found out the editor was looking for an author to write on this topic, so I submitted a proposal."
"I have always had a desire to offer something to help teens in the exciting yet oftentimes challenging transition into adulthood."
"I am a writer, and this was an opportunity to write."

While those reasons are definitely true, I left out one of the most important reasons I wrote on "this topic." But I want to tell *you*.

I grew up not understanding substance abuse. I remember the feelings that I had around people who had drug or alcohol problems. Out of naivety, I judged them in ways that benefitted no one.

And then, as I began growing up, little by little, I started to realize that someone in my life might have a problem with substance abuse. At first I denied. And then other people close to this person and I denied together. But eventually, we realized we couldn't keep pretending we didn't see. Along the path of addiction this person almost died. Watching this was like being behind a glass wall, witnessing someone you love suffer; being so close, yet not being able to reach out and help.

Pretty soon it was obvious that the only thing we could do to reach this person was to break the glass. That meant getting rid of the barrier that kept us all from facing the addiction. It meant seeking answers and finding a key that would open the door to well-being.

It might seem odd that we questioned doing this. But we were worried that if we were wrong about our suspicions that this person had a substance abuse issue, it would seem we lacked trust. But finally, we had no choice. We confronted this person.

Watching someone you love struggle with a substance use disorder is like being behind a glass wall.

We struggled a lot during the years, not knowing how to help, worrying, while hoping. But I am certain, without a doubt, it was nothing compared to the pain, struggles, guilt, confusion, fear, and despair that this person went through. At the time, we did not fully understand it all. Mostly, though, we felt helpless.

I was very private about this situation, and most people in my life did not realize I was struggling with this because I did not share. It wasn't until I confided in another close friend that I realized how prevalent problems like this really are, and I don't just mean in general around the country, but in our own neighborhoods and towns and schools. I learned how sharing with others for support instead of dealing with it alone can make such a difference.

That was years ago. The person I speak of is now stable, and I'm wiser on the subject. My prejudices were shattered once I realized that substance abuse is also like an epidemic and touches almost all of us, in one way or another, either by association or personal connections like the one I had.

That leads me to my final reason for writing this book: to offer honesty, insights, and hope to those teens who decide to read this book. To those teens who have gone down the path of substance use and abuse, as well as those who haven't yet and never will. I'm writing it for my own kids and their friends. This is for those who were once teens and have gone through substance-related issues. I'm writing it for all of you who I may never meet. Everyone who lives in society is subject to this issue somehow affecting them. I write this for you.

So throughout this book, I hope to shed light on the subject of addictions, substances, the process of becoming addicted, and the methods of getting help. When this book is in the hands of readers, one of the outcomes that I wish for is that it helps to break down biases against people who are dealing with this disorder.

Another is to empower readers. To empower teens. To empower *you.* The process of empowering includes understanding, which then leads to the concept that when you come upon a locked door, keep seeking until you find one you can open. You have the key.

I hope this book helps to open up your mind.

Because of the many learning opportunities, I have developed a new perspective, and I know that these experiences are what helped to fuel my passion for writing the book you hold in your hands. Though I had a tremendous amount of passion for this project, I have to admit I struggled at times to write it. The more research I did, the more people I talked with, the more I realized what an enormous topic this really is. There were times when I would stare at the computer screen and wonder what words would really have any impact on someone who is in the downward spiral of addiction. Or what sentences strung together could have any influence on teens who have already heard their moms and dads, their teachers, their religious leaders remind them to "just say no." But then I would remind myself of the people who came forth (see acknowledgments and contributors)—all of those who responded to my request to meet with me, offer their expertise, share their personal life stories, help edit the book, and talk through the various issues within it that needed attention. These folks gave me a new enriched perspective. They inspired me to realize that even if this book isn't a magic source to help you and other teens blast through the peer-pressure years unscathed—if this book becomes just a simple tool that is real and honest—you will know that all of those people who contributed, including me, are a part of a reservoir of knowledge, experiences, wisdom, and mostly love that you can tap into *knowing you aren't alone.* Whether you are involved with substances or not,

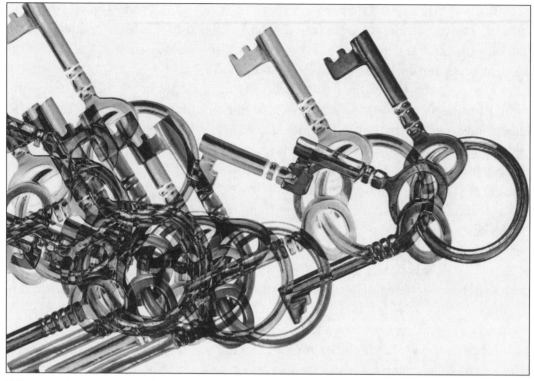

When you come upon a locked door, keep seeking until you find one you can open. You have the key.

Like the basketball team, like an orchestra, like the writing of a book—it takes a group of people working toward the same cause.

if you are a teen, this book is for you. Like the basketball team, like an orchestra, like the writing of a book—it takes a group of people working toward the same cause.

I've learned that a topic like this brings people together even more than it separates. And if we are honest and true, it will unify us, helping us to help each other. The process of writing this book helped me to realize this. I am eternally grateful for this opportunity to share with you.

I hope that the process of reading this book inspires in you the desire for taking apart paradigms; for questions that keep you searching, for new perspectives, and for opportunities yet to unfold.

Preface

"When your view on the world and your intellect are being challenged and you begin to feel uncomfortable because of a contradiction you've detected that is threatening your current model of the world . . . pay attention. You are about to learn something."
—*William H. Drury, novelist and poet*

Substance abuse disorder. It has gotten the attention of experts, parents, and teachers. It has gotten the attention of YOU.

There's good reason. It is a vast topic and one that is loaded with many feelings, facts, and philosophies. Plus, substances are all around us. You turn on the TV, listen to music, page through magazines, read books, surf the Internet . . . references to drugs and alcohol seem to be everywhere. And it isn't just the references that are everywhere; drugs and alcohol seem to be everywhere, too.

This book covers the scope of this disorder by providing a clear, honest delivery of the information about substances. By the way, as I've mentioned in the previous part of the book, the pages you'll read contain a lot of quotes and insights from a lot of sources. I fully believe that it's great to hear things from people who've been there, done that, or studied and know a lot about that. Plus, it's kinda cool when one resource backs up another. I've reached out and found some really great experts willing to share with you. Not only from those whose job it is to focus on substance use disorders, but others with different perspectives as well. Bottom line is, you won't just be hearing from me.

Speaking of reading things from different people, you'll also read things in different ways. What do I mean? I mean that some of the stuff is really scientific, for those of you who like the facts and stats. Some of it comes in the form of personal stories, for those of you who are drawn to the real-life snapshots. You'll see artwork by teens like you, for those who appreciate the story behind the drawing. Some of this book is even shared as quotes from all different folks—philosophers and writers and pop stars and even religious and spiritual leaders. Wait—are we going to get religious here? Nope . . . but some of you may respond to the words of these leaders in our world, so that's all here too.

There's a little bit for everyone. And a lot for you all. And the most for those who have an open mind.

Let's look at a summary of the chapters and what you can expect to read in each.

Chapter 1: "Pre–Substance Exposure"—This is the time before a teen is exposed to or tempted to try a substance. What could be said about that? You'll learn some interesting facts about the brain.

Chapter 2: "Experimenting with Substances"—This experimentation time could range anywhere from a sip of beer to a puff of a cigarette to other types of drugs. But what is involved with the temptation to try?

Chapter 3: "Increased Substance Use/Prevention of Addiction"—This chapter deals with the concept of teens using on a more regular basis, how he or she feels about it, what happens to the body and brain, and how this use might lead to the subject of the next chapter.

Chapter 4: "Addiction"—This chapter gives honest insights into substance disorders. You'll get the facts but you'll also get the feelings from teens who have or have had substance disorders.

Chapter 5: "Recovery/Relapse"—You'll learn some information here that I bet you didn't realize about recovery.

Chapter 6: "Holistic Methods"—You'll read some great information about all kinds of methods and approaches to recovery that are pretty natural.

Chapter 7: "More to Think About"—This chapter has more good stuff, insights from professionals, words from teens, thoughts from people with jobs you might someday want yourself . . . don't miss this one.

Chapter 8: "From the Perspective of . . ."—This chapter has some honest thoughts from folks who share their views on teens and this issue of substance use and abuse. Ever wondered how a mom feels when she knows her son has a drug problem? This chapter has a few perspectives that you'll find worth reading.

"The End"—Each book must come to an end, and this chapter shares thoughts about the ending and where this may lead you.

Appendixes A, B, C, D—These appendixes contains lists of resources, books, movies, contributors who shared for the book, and artwork done by teens. Take a look. It's pretty interesting. And inspiring.

Index—The index has relevant terms or names that might be of interest to you, the reader, to help you find more about the terms or names within the book.

About the Author—Yes, just what it says; it has information about the author.

Besides knowing what is in the book, I also thought you might find it helpful to know how the book is organized. That seems pretty boring, but I want you to know that this isn't like a regular textbook where you can just scan the text in bold and then answer the true and false. I obviously want this book to be a useful tool for you, so by using it a certain way, I believe it will be. You might be tempted to page through or flip to the chapters that sound the most interesting to you. You might be drawn to the photos or artwork (maybe you are a picture-book fan at heart) and want to skip to those. Mostly, it might not appeal to you to sit down and start at the beginning and read page by page. Reading a textbook from cover to cover? Cleaning your room might seem better compared to a night with a textbook.

Hold on, don't close the book covers yet. I used to be a teen once, so I get it. That's why I wrote this book so that it is set up kind of like a novel or a movie. The tension increases as you go along. There are characters (real ones). There are sad parts, happy parts, maybe some confusing parts. And in the end, you'll find out what happens to the "good guys." (Ha! What do I mean by that?) Start at the beginning (right here!) and keep reading through.

A Few Points That Set the Groundwork

First off, are teens the only ones affected by substance abuse? Obviously not. According to the National Institute on Drug Abuse, "People of all ages suffer the harmful consequences of drug abuse and addiction."

Babies in the womb can be exposed when the mom is involved in substances.
Adolescents (sorry to talk about you in third person) are affected, and of course we'll focus more on this soon.
Adults who are addicted are affected; it can affect every aspect of their lives.[1]

Wait a second. Isn't this book supposed to be for and about teens? Why is there mention of everybody else, like babies? Like adults? The answer is simple: you either were one (a baby), will have one (a baby), and/or will be one (an adult). So be prepared to hear from adults who were teens, who tried substances around the same age you are now, and how it affected their lives even after they graduated from the teen years.

By the way, you might discover that once in a while something is repeated in this book, and you'll read something that you've read before. I do this intentionally. You remember why. You're smart.

As I was writing this book, the American Psychiatric Association was preparing to put out its next edition of the *Diagnostic and Statistical Manual of Mental Disorders* (*DSM*), a rather thick, very textbookish resource. The terms I use in this book are used for the sake of simplicity. By the time you are reading this,

> ### ? What Is Addiction According to the National Institute of Drug Abuse (NIDA)?
>
> "Addiction is defined as a chronic, relapsing brain disease that is characterized by compulsive drug seeking and use, despite harmful consequences. It is considered a brain disease because drugs change the brain—they change its structure and how it works. These brain changes can be long lasting, and can lead to the harmful behaviors seen in people who abuse drugs."[2]
>
> That's right, teens; addiction is a nine-letter word that packs a big punch. It can knock the breath out of you—permanently!
>
> "Addiction is similar to other diseases, such as heart disease. Both disrupt the normal, healthy functioning of the underlying organ, have serious harmful consequences, are preventable, treatable, and if left untreated, can last a lifetime."[3]

there may be different terms used. For the most updated information, please refer to the latest edition of the *DSM*.

Let's give an overview of the types of substances we'll be referring to throughout the book. (No quiz on this later, but it's good to know what's out there.) These definitions are from NIDA. Also, look in the section of this book titled "Appendix A: More Facts at a Glance," for . . . well, yes, for more facts.

Anabolic steroids: Anabolic steroids are artificial versions of a hormone that's in all of us—testosterone. Some people take anabolic steroid pills or injections to try to build muscle faster.

Cocaine: Cocaine is made from the leaf of the coca plant. It often comes in the form of a white powder that some people inhale through their nose. Another form of cocaine, known as crack, can be smoked.

Hallucinogens: Hallucinogens cause people to experience—you guessed it—hallucinations, imagined experiences that seem real.

Inhalants: Hair spray, gasoline, spray paint—they are all inhalants, and so are lots of other everyday products. Some people inhale the vapors on purpose.

Marijuana: You may have heard it called pot, weed, grass, ganja, or skunk, but marijuana by any other name is still a drug that affects the brain.

Methamphetamine: Methamphetamine comes in many different forms and is snorted, swallowed, injected, or smoked. Methamphetamine can cause lots of harmful effects, including inability to sleep, paranoia, aggressiveness, and hallucinations.

Opiates: Maybe you've heard of drugs called heroin, morphine, or codeine. These are examples of opiates. If someone uses opiates again and again, his or her brain is likely to become dependent on them.

Prescription drug abuse: Abuse is when someone takes a prescription drug without a doctor's prescription or in a way or amount that is different from what was prescribed. Abuse of prescription drugs can have serious and harmful health effects, including poisoning and even death.

Tobacco addiction: When tobacco is smoked, nicotine is absorbed by the lungs and quickly moved into the bloodstream, where it is circulated throughout the brain.[4]

Now that you have at least a basic understanding of some of the types of substances, let's turn the page and begin at the beginning. No matter what your reason is for picking up this book, it is important you read it. Remember, no one is immune to being touched some way or another by substance issues. Equip yourself with information that can eventually turn to knowledge. Go ahead, find a quiet place, sit down, and begin reading.

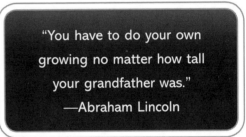

"You have to do your own growing no matter how tall your grandfather was."
—Abraham Lincoln

Notes

1. NIDA, "Drugs, Brains, and Behavior: The Science of Addiction," http://www.drugabuse .gov/publications/science-addiction/introduction (accessed December 2012).
2. NIDA, "The Science of Drug Abuse and Addiction," http://www.drugabuse.gov/publications/ media-guide/science-drug-abuse-addiction (accessed December 2012).
3. NIDA, "Drugs, Brains, and Behavior: The Science of Addiction," http://www.drugabuse .gov/publications/science-addiction/drug-abuse-addiction (accessed December 2012).
4. NIDA, "Drugs of Abuse," www.drugabuse.gov/drugs-abuse (accessed December 2012).

Acknowledgments

I've come to discover that nothing in life is really accomplished alone. There is always an exchange of energy, knowledge, or resources.

It is certainly true of this book. This resource is the culmination of not only my efforts, but also those of many others.

Thank you to the publishing house, Scarecrow Press, where the idea for this book was inspired. Scarecrow Press is made up of a team of experts that work together on each book. One such expert on the team that an author works the closest with is her editor. Editors are more than just folks who circle spelling mistakes with a red pen, and my editor, Arlene, has been an asset to this book since we first discussed the concept. Often editors are writers themselves and share their unique talents on a writing project to make it the best it can be. Such is the case with Arlene.

Special thanks to the readers and supporters: Mike Nichols, who spot-checked the manuscript, giving his expert input. My critique groups, who from the beginning inspired me to pour my heart into this project. My writing friends—those that took the time to listen to a paragraph here, a sentence there, a concept, a page, a chapter. My brothers and sister and my parents, for being there along the way. My family, for their endless support and for taking on more when I had to do less. Thank you for understanding my need to do this project.

To you all . . . I'm grateful.

A nonfiction book is made up of facts that are gathered and culminated from reports and research referenced from other sources. There were many professionals who agreed to help with this book, either by meeting with me, fact-checking for me, talking on the phone, or sharing information in another form—people like John Mabry, who put his research hat back on and dug deep to find the most current and up-to-date information out there. And Dr. Ryan Byrne, who shared his expertise in certain facts and details in the book. A special thank you to Dr. Gabor Maté, physician, public speaker, and author, who took the time to offer his insights to teens, and Pandit Rajmani Tigunait, spiritual head of the Himalayan Institute. Please know that I am grateful for your contributions and that your input will make a positive impact.

This book also contains contributions from many people who shared insights, experiences, and wisdom. Some shared direct experiences that they lived through, others shared about attributes needed in careers, still others their perspective on substance abuse.

In addition to those whom I dealt directly with, I thank those who will remain nameless—a collective part of a whole of the information gathered and shared by the vast reservoir of knowledge that we can all tap into. Resources and organizations like the Ozaukee County Sheriff's Department and all of those who I worked with at the police departments, pamphlets about substance abuse available to the public, and websites that share research. But additionally there are the contributors who were the forefathers and mothers of this topic, helping by offering the earliest research on substance abuse. I learned by reading everything I could get my hands on. I learned also by listening to someone who learned from someone else . . . as is what happens with knowledge through the trail of time. Thank you, too, to those out there who were teachers to me in one way or another, or still are. You've helped me see life from different angles and mostly have helped me to see myself as a clearer version of who I am. This has allowed me to write this book from an honest perspective.

The presence of all of these people—those I know and those I don't, but all of whom are teachers in some way—is important, and I acknowledge and thank you for your place in this project. Any information that I claim to be my original work, while written from my own experience, is in some way attributed to others who have added to and contributed to that reservoir of knowledge and wisdom.

There is a special group of people to whom I offer a deep gratitude: those who have shared what it is like to be involved in substance use and abuse. They have opened up and told personal stories that involve love, pain, and suffering and in some cases tragedy and in others, triumph. Sharing our own trials and successes makes us vulnerable. It is my hope that this sharing not only helps the readers, but also helps the writers to find peace knowing that their involvement in this book will be helping others. And that their contribution in sharing what they've gone through or are going through, is making a positive, and lasting, difference. Thank you.

Finally, a special thank you to the teens reading this book—thank you for striving to stay true . . . *to being you.*

Live Your Light.

PRE-SUBSTANCE EXPOSURE

....

"To be yourself in a world that is constantly trying to make you something else is the greatest accomplishment."—Ralph Waldo Emerson, American essayist and poet who was seen as a champion of individualism

Unless someone is born an addict, there is a time in each person's life before he or she is ever exposed to or experiments with substances. Many children have heard about and have been warned against drugs, alcohol, and tobacco use, and by the time these children reach the teenage years, many still will not have been tempted to try a substance themselves. But often, the same kids who eventually end up experimenting with substances believed at one time that they would never try.

This chapter deals with that "pre" time, a time before any substances have entered a teen's body and before making the decision to try has entered his or her thoughts. This material covers scientific research that talks about brain development and how this development may play a part in a teenager's choice making. You will also read some real-life teen stories.

As you probably already know, especially if you've read the beginning of this book, the topic of substance use disorders is extensive, complicated, and confusing and it can be scary and lonely. But keep reading because the more information you have, the more empowered you will be. Often, the facts about these substances aren't known by the user when he or she decides to try. So learn all that you can so you can make informed decisions. If you are beyond that point with your experiences with substances, I suggest you still take in the words within these pages. Often new knowledge can play an important role.

Teens Who Experiment

So what are the reasons a teen might decide to try a substance? Besides not knowing about the full dangers of substance use, there are other reasons why teens might experiment. Even though you are a teen yourself and might have some of the answers, let's see what the professional feels about the variety of reasons teens may be tempted to experiment with substances.

Young people may choose to use because of peer pressure, feelings of boredom, or a belief that drugs will help them excel in sports, on stage, or in social

Some people take drugs because they believe drugs will enhance their performance.

settings. Sometimes it is to boost self-esteem or to relieve stress, anxiety, or even depression. Teens may try a substance simply out of curiosity or to not be left out of what everyone else is doing. They not only don't want to be left out, they also don't want to be left out of the time after everyone did something, the aftermath time when teens talk and discuss about what they've experienced together.

Just as each teen is unique, each reason behind the choice is unique to the teen who says yes.

Therefore, when we discuss substance use and abuse as a teen and start with the question, What makes one teen say yes and another say no? it is probably obvious that many factors play into the decision. According to the National Institute on Drug Abuse (NIDA),[1] people begin to take drugs for a variety of reasons:

- To feel good. Many drugs can elicit strong pleasure feelings, so people take them to feel good. And these feelings can vary from drug to drug. Some cause feelings of relaxation. Some produce feelings of excitement and feelings of euphoria.
- To stop feeling badly. If they are depressed, stressed, or have social anxiety, people might choose to take drugs to make themselves feel better.
- To do better in school, on tests, even in athletics. They believe drugs enhance their performance.

Of course, as mentioned earlier, some people take substances out of curiosity. What does it feel like to take it, try it? If others are doing it, they may be curious to understand why.

Could the actual development of the person influence his or her decisions? Could another factor—other than willpower, the desire to be or feel better, or curiosity—play a role in saying yes or no?

The Teen's Healthy and Astounding Brain

We know that the brain is obviously a major organ in the body, but why is a whole section of almost every chapter of this book devoted to the brain?

When it comes to substances that enter the body, the brain enters the story in a big way. This first section about the brain discusses the brain *not* on drugs.

Some of you may think reading about anatomy type stuff is a yawner, but come on—this is about that mysterious body part that is enabling you to read and understand what you are reading right now. Isn't it important you understand it a bit? You could read books and books about the brain and still not have all of the information. We'll share just a tad about this organ and hope that if you find it interesting, you'll do more research on your own.

And later on, when we talk about what drugs do to the brain, it will help you absorb it all better if you first know how your brain works naturally. So, read on.

The human brain (the one located in your head) is one of the most complex organs in the body. This white-and-gray, three-pound (give or take) mass of matter helps with all of your activity. You need it to eat, sleep, breathe, laugh with a friend, and write a song. It is, in a way, like a computer, accepting incoming information, organizing it, and responding. Made up of many parts, the brain works as a unit and is responsible for your thoughts, feelings, and actions. If you think about it, it's obvious that the functions the brain carries out are critical.

So What about the Effects of Drugs on This Life-Sustaining Organ?

"Drugs can alter important brain areas that are necessary for life-sustaining functions and can drive the compulsive drug abuse that marks addiction."[2] Well, that statement pretty much sums it up, doesn't it? Why go on and on about the brain when we already know that drugs can damage it? Danger can come in all shapes and sizes. Perhaps it would be wise to learn a bit more about your own brain before we learn what exactly those drugs would do to it.

The Cerebral Cortex, Limbic System, and the Brain Stem

Raise your hand if you know what the brain stem is responsible for. Come on, really, raise your hand. No one is watching. Well, whether you followed those directions or not, your brain was firing just from reading those words. The brain stem, which links the brain with the spinal cord and runs down the back, has nerves that run through it. It lets the brain know what's going on in the body and, while doing so, handles essential living functions.

But what about that feeling you had when I asked you to raise your hand? Let's hear it for the limbic system, which sets our emotional responses and links together a collection of brain structures. Remember the last time you had a warm chocolate chip cookie? Mmmm. Those feel-good feelings start right in the limbic system. This good-feeling place encourages us to repeat behaviors that feel good. (Foreshadowing . . . you've learned about this term in school, right?)

Trivia question: What takes up about three-fourths of the entire brain and looks like a gray mushroom? If you answered the limbic system, *beep*, try again. The real answer is . . . the cerebral cortex. This grand part of the body is split up into four lobes, and each of these lobes is responsible for the interplay of specific functions. Some are responsible for processing information transmitted from our senses, which translates to us seeing, feeling, hearing, smelling, and tasting. The frontal cortex (guess where this is located), also known as the forebrain, is sometimes called the thinking center. And while other parts of the brain are involved with behavior and emotion, this is the master area that gives us the ability to think, plan, and problem-solve and is involved with emotional control. (More foreshadowing. Are you putting the puzzle together?)

The anterior cingulate gyrus (ACG) is a part of the brain that helps people see options in life, enabling them to be flexible in situations and shift gears. Some research indicates that among other factors, ACG imbalance may be related to addiction disorders.

So that's all well and good, but then what? There are all these great parts of the brain and all these important functions but how does your mind read the words "raise your hand," and your hand then actually rises? *It's all about communication.*

How Does the Brain Communicate?

A master power center of communication, the brain is made up of billions of neurons that we can also call nerve cells. These neurons form networks (think World Wide Web and cell phones) and they pass messages to and from those different parts of the brain, as well as the spinal column and the peripheral nervous system (think friends communicating through e-mails, Facebook, texting, etc.). So these nerve networks regulate and coordinate how we act and how we feel.

So, hold on cowboy or girl; how many nerve cells did we say the brain is made up of? Billions, right? Well each one of these sends and receives messages through impulses, namely, electrical impulses. Once one of these cells gets a message, it processes it and then sends it to other neurons. Again, let's think of the cell phone and how we receive a text, then send it on to another cell phone. There's nothing like a "cell" to pass on a message (lol).

What carries these messages from one nerve (neuron) cell to another? you ask. I'm so glad you did. Here is the answer. And it's a cool word to remember: *neurotransmitters.* These are the brain's chemical messengers. These chemical messengers are responsible for passing the messages between neurons.

We have the transmitters, but how about the receivers? Neurotransmitters attach to specialized sites on the receiving cell, and guess what these are called? Yep, receptors. And each neurotransmitter goes together with its receptor like a "key and lock." (Note that research is ongoing, and "neurons in different pathways will often have different types of receptors in a given family."[3]) This helps to make sure that the appropriate message is forwarded on. Maybe like typing in the code of your friend's phone number that sends the text message to your friend's phone instead of your mom's phone. (That's a relief!)

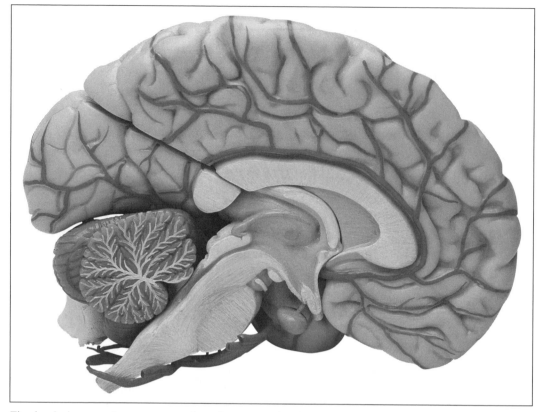

The brain is a master power center of communication.

Finally, there is something called the brain's chemical recyclers, which are the transporters. "Located on the cell that releases the neurotransmitter, transporters recycle these neurotransmitters (i.e., bringing them back into the cell that released them), thereby shutting off the signal between neurons."[4]

Do you kind of understand now how the brain works in a general way? How the parts work together to allow you to breathe, swallow, think, smile, run, and think? (I know, I said "think" twice in that list but it made you think twice, didn't it?) So imagine, your brain is this amazing collection of billions of cells all working together to create . . . *you*! It's like an intricate network functioning to balance complex systems in the body. Balanced, that is, until something comes in to throw it off balance. More to come on this.

There is a little known secret about your brain that would be good for you to find out about. And right about now. You know how your body is changing and you are starting to look like an adult? You might be done growing taller, but guess what hasn't finished growing? Yep, you guessed it, your brain.

It was once thought that the brain was fully developed at an early age. Researchers now believe, through a study using MRI (magnetic resonance imaging) on the brain at various ages, that the brain isn't fully developed until the person reaches his or her mid to upper twenties. It is the "higher-order" brain centers, like the prefrontal cortex, that aren't completely developed until early adulthood. What does this tell us about teens, and how does this relate to substance use and abuse issues?

The frontal lobes, responsible for problem solving and reasoning and for slowing the desire for thrills and risk taking, develop last. Remember that fore-shadowing? Think about this: when a teenager is confronted with many critical choices, his or her capacity to make decisions that would keep him or her from being involved in risky activities is less developed than an adult's, especially when the teen is under stress. So what does that mean really? It means this: you, as a teen, don't have the brain of an adult yet, plain and simple. We aren't talking in-telligence. We aren't talking fashion sense. Seriously, we are talking the ability to make sound decisions that would protect you and keep you safe. You don't have the ability you will have when you reach your upper twenties. And by the way, this isn't some scare tactic. This is fact.

As a teen yourself, after reading this, you might begin to wonder about your own ability to make decisions that are the best for your own welfare. (Maybe it at least crosses your mind?) What is important to understand is simply that during the teenage years, one part of the brain is more developed than another part.

When you were still a young child, your parent would perhaps guard you as you crossed the street, holding your hand, making sure you were not hit by a car. At that early age, you did not have the capacity to fully understand the concept of the danger of a car hitting you. So no matter how many times your parents would say, "Be careful when you cross the street," still, if you were chasing a red ball that was rolling across the street, you could not heed that warning as an older person could. Your brain simply could not process the danger like an adult could. Now, I'm not suggesting your brain is like that of a toddler. It is, of course, more developed. I'm simply suggesting what the facts make clear—that teens don't have the brain they will have later on to make decisions they may be being faced with, similar to a toddler not having the ability to make decisions about chasing a ball into the road. This affects teens' ability to make sound decisions. Even decid-ing about making decisions is impinged upon. Think twice about that one.

When an adult gives you rules to follow, though you may feel like you are old enough to make decisions on your own (and for many decisions you are), there are times when you still need your parent or guardian to "hold your hand." Some adults realize that when a teen is confronted with the option to try drugs, the part of the brain that would normally say, "No, that isn't a good idea. It is against the law. It is bad for me. It isn't a choice I want to make," isn't as developed as the part of the brain that says, "That sounds like an exciting time, and if I do this, I'll fit in with the other kids! Yay! Everyone is doing it; if it isn't hurting them, why would it hurt me?! Yay!" These are the adults who might most vehemently

Ways to Equip Yourself to Stay Clean

When you ask yourself whether you know ways to keep yourself safe, see if you come up with the following solutions:

Only go to houses where the parents are home. Kids are less likely to get in trouble under adult supervision.

Don't go into a situation where you know people will be engaging in at-risk behaviors.

Don't hang around people you feel intimidated by, people you know can influence you, especially at times where you think they may push you to do something you otherwise would not want to do.

Older teens often have influence over younger; keep that in mind when hanging out with kids older than you.

Listen to your intuition. If you feel funny deep in your gut, avoid and do something else.

When posed with a choice to engage in at-risk behavior with substances, consider these questions:

What will this do to my body?

What will this do to my brain?

How might this affect the feelings I have toward myself?

Am I willing to lose the trust of those who trust me to make the right choice?

Am I willing to lose privileges like being on a sports team?

Is this what I would want my younger sibling to know I'm doing?

This is breaking the law; am I ready to face the consequences?

What if this one-time try hooks me, and I become addicted?

What does that little voice inside me say?

So hang on to this list or one you have created (maybe store it in the memory bank of your brain) and have it with you the next time you find yourself on your own with your still-developing brain.

try to provide teens with alternative options that would keep teens out of scenarios where they have to make decisions that are challenging for them to make. If you've got one of these adults around, keep 'em around. They know (usually) what's good for you. Nonetheless, most likely, you'll be faced with choices that you'll have to make on your own.

Knowing about this scientific evidence on the developing brain, how could you protect yourself? When you are confronted with an at-risk choice, will you take pause and step back, seeing your choice from a different perspective? Even better, perhaps you could navigate yourself away from being confronted with such choices to begin with? Having the knowledge that your brain isn't as developed as it will be doesn't leave you room for excuses, but rather gives you a tool to help you realize that if you are in certain situations, especially those that are stressful, you may make choices you wouldn't otherwise make if you had the brain development of an older person. These same choices, however, may have an impact on your future, so it is up to you to take on the responsibility and avoid these situations.

Body Development

Now that you've got a better understanding about your brain development, let's talk a bit about your bod. As mentioned, you are starting to look like an adult. Your body is changing and changing quickly. Or not quickly enough. Oftentimes those changes (or lack thereof) can throw you off balance emotionally.

Though you can't feel your brain developing, you can feel how your body develops, especially when hormones start to ramp up and get into the game. Teens' bodies go through a tremendous change as they reach puberty. Hormones can affect not only body changes but mood as well. These changes can leave some teens feeling self-conscious about their bodies, and they may be comparing their figures to others or to the images they see in the media. Dealing with the changes of their bodies and the insecurities that these changes may be causing may increase the need for teens to want to fit in. So let's repeat this again, looking at it another way: *know what your attitude is and become aware of how you are feeling about yourself before you put yourself in a situation that may beg you to make a difficult choice in front of your peers.* Do you see how this all comes together? (Or if you aren't prepared, could fall apart?)

Pressures

As a teen you have many pressures. This is as much a fact as the brain development stuff we discussed. It sometimes seems like demands on teens are ramping up to

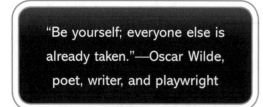

"Be yourself; everyone else is already taken."—Oscar Wilde, poet, writer, and playwright

high and dangerous levels. Depending upon each teen's circumstances, teens may face pressures that put them at added risk for the feelings of needing a break or an escape. These pressures may include the need to do well in school, to score well on the ACT, to prepare for future college or employment, as well as the pressure to get a job and earn money. A teen may experience the need to excel at a sport, to volunteer for community service hours, keep up with homework, attend family functions, socialize, and uphold family responsibilities; the list can go on and on. And this is all while dealing with changes in one's own moods and body and dealing with the desire to fit in. Sound familiar? More importantly, does this *feel* familiar? All of these pressures of the fast-paced life can make teens more vulnerable and more apt to seek relief. Even to "self-medicate." Know this. Be in tune to what you are going through. Understand that there are many alternative solutions to relieving this stress (see more on this in chapter 6). Protect yourself.

You may relate to those feelings of "I would never try alcohol or drugs." Like I mentioned at the beginning of this chapter, none of the teens (save for one who was growing up before the dangers of tobacco were discovered) that I interviewed said they had planned on becoming a user; not one said that as a child or moving into the teen years, he or she thought he or she would try later on.

Janis Kinens, a pastor living in a small town in the Midwest says, "I don't think anyone 'always knew they would do drugs.' I think there are a myriad of complex 'triggers' including both genetic as well as environmental factors."[5]

How Does Our Environment Contribute to the Likelihood of Drug or Alcohol Use?

According to some research, if a teen has grown up in an environment where family members partake in drug abuse, the likelihood of teen substance abuse increases. Watching a behavior over and over by those people you deem as your role models might make the behavior seem acceptable and normal. Can you relate to these feelings?

Social Media

It isn't surprising to find out that some studies report that heavy use of social media correlates to use of alcohol, cigarettes, and other drugs. Not only can the use

Some studies report that heavy use of social media correlates to use of alcohol, cigarettes, and other drugs.

of various types of communication become addictive, the pressures through the lightning fast transfer of information about peers brings the concept of peer pressure to a new level. Teens can keep track of what other teens are doing, thinking, and saying, almost as the action occurs. The need to fit in has never been so high. But social media streams aren't the only factor related to a teen experimenting.

Pressure from Your Peers

Despite the often daunting pressures that it seems adults put on teens, there is a fair amount of pressures teens put on themselves and even more that teens put onto other teens. Some forms of peer pressure could be defined as bullying. Have you ever felt pressure that makes you feel less than you are in order to manipulate you into doing what your peer wants you to do? Do you ever fall prey to these pressures? It doesn't even have to be about drugs or alcohol. What about your friends just encouraging you to do something that "isn't you," like staying out after curfew, watching a movie you know you aren't supposed to, even cheating on a test? Do you ever say yes just because it is easier than saying no? Have you ever put these kinds of pressures on your friends or other teenagers? These pressures can lead to succumbing to more dangerous pressures, like being pressured to go to a party where you know there will be drinking.

Let's face it . . . teens can make being the job of being a teenager really hard.

Is There More to Peer Pressure Than Meets the Eye?

So what makes a kid begin to care more about what fellow peers think than their own parents? It seems only natural that children, as they grow into teens, become more aware of their peers and what their peers may think. And to you, as a teen, it probably seems as natural as breathing. Stay tuned to learn more about this. First, let's figure out what you think about using substances.

What *Is* Your Attitude about Drinking? Taking Drugs? Smoking?

According to Donna Bestor Krieger, former coordinator of the Alliance for a Drug-Free Wisconsin, "Pre-teens see substance use all around them—in movies, TV, with their parents and friends. Therefore, it is a part of their everyday lives, and they aren't concerned about it. (Unless someone close to them is addicted and causing harmful behavior.) They may think using is a 'rite of passage,' that is, having a few beers gives them a sense of power, feeling more grown-up."[6]

So if you feel like substance use is just a common thing, what would motivate you to change your whole perception of use? If you do feel that using is what everyone is doing, and it isn't a big deal, what will make you see otherwise? Consider this: millions of dollars and thousands of professionals are dedicated to answering that question. This is not a casual little problem people are playing with. There is a reason why books like this are written. Substance addiction is a disease. *It kills people.* How do you feel when you read that statement? How do you feel about trying or using substances as a teen?

Thoughts from Teens

The following section of this chapter is dedicated to contributions from young people who have agreed to share their own personal stories for the book. They all shared with the hopes that what they have gone through might, in some way, help others.

"Wait a second here," you might be saying. "Aren't we supposed to be careful about being influenced by teens?" Of course. You should always think for yourself. So read these stories and see what you can learn from them. Just like you would learn a lot about yourself (and your friend) if you turned down an invitation to a party because you knew it was going to put you at risk, you, too, can learn from others' experiences as well. When you are reading the stories, note the differences between them but also the similarities.

By the way, some of the people who shared their stories are now adults. We felt it important to hear from people who had different experiences to learn how substance use affected not only their lives as teens, but their entire lives. And also, please know, as mentioned at the beginning of the book, that some of the people who shared their stories chose to remain anonymous. Some used their own names. All told their stories from their hearts. Imagine the strength this took. You'll see. What you'll read here is the start of each story. In each chapter, the stories will progress based on what the chapter is about. So in this chapter, you'll read about these teenagers during the "pre–experimental stage" of their teenage lives. In the next chapter, you'll read about the exact same people during the next stage, the "first exposure" to substances. Take note, you might begin to care about these characters. Remember, they aren't fictitious. These people are real. As real as you and me.

Personal Stories

Lily

She begins her story as a middle school student:

> "Always be a first-rate version of yourself and not a second-rate version of someone else."—Judy Garland, movie star who played "Dorothy" in *The Wizard of OZ*, had a barbiturate addiction, and died of an overdose of sleeping pills

I'm Lily, an eighth grader, and I have never been involved with drugs or alcohol. I think this is partially because my friends don't do drugs and I'm not into big parties. Two of my goals are to be healthy and go to college and I know drugs wouldn't help me, so I've tried to stay clear of them. It makes me proud to be able to say that I've never made that mistake. Although some might think it makes you look cool, kids at my school look down on others that drink or do drugs. They aren't as likely to hang out with the people that do drugs because they don't want to get involved. The people at my school that do drugs don't do well in school and hang out together. This shows that it's important to surround yourself by people you look up to. Whether you realize it or not, you will be influenced by the people you spend time with, either with your attitude or choices you make.[7]

Lon

He begins his story as a middle school student:

> I'm 14 years old and live a pretty average life. I go to the local middle school and live at home with my mom, dad, and two sisters. I have great friends who are great influences on me. The town I live in is small and super nice and quiet. I always feel completely safe. Would I ever do drugs? No. I think no one ever plans to take drugs. It almost seems accidental. It seems like people feel so sad that there is no other way to be happy. I'm happy with my friends and family and life and I would never want to screw that up.[8]

Brian

He begins his story as a middle school student:

> Growing up my parents always taught me what was wrong and right. It was never a question about drinking; I knew I would never try it or even think about it. When I entered middle school, I got very scared and nervous that my friends would peer pressure me into trying stuff and doing things my parents would not want me doing. I thought about it every day and my mom promised me we would get through it together.[9]

Carol

She begins her story as a college student:

> I grew up before research started finding out how bad smoking was for you. My mom smoked as did all the people on TV and in the movies so I thought I probably would. I probably didn't start until I was in college because I was pretty sure my parents would not approve.[10]

Tim

He begins his story as a high school student:

> I had many opportunities to drink as a teen. I never did because of my sisters. They were older and they were both in treatment centers and so I didn't want to go down the path that they did. I was afraid because I had seen people fall apart.[11]

Brady

He begins his story as a high school student:

I always thought, "never do it." I always focused on soccer. That was my natural high.[12]

Kyle

He begins his story as a high school student:

Before I even used or even tried drugs or alcohol I told myself I would never try or even attempt to use them. I told myself it was poison for the body. I never even thought about using or doing drugs seeing my number one dream was to go into the Army. When I was a kid and seen other kids on drugs or alcohol it pretty much made me think they were lowlifes and had nothing going for them in life.[13]

Princess Peach

She begins her story as a middle school student:

Did I think I would ever try drugs of alcohol? Obviously, of course like most of us, no.[14]

Jessica

She begins her story as a middle school student:

I grew up in a small, quiet town in the southwest. I had a great family. Mom and Dad, and two brothers that I got along with. I spent a lot of my time in the performing arts. Like many little kids, I started dance classes before I started school. From a young age, I danced hard and I was good. I stood out from the others as one of the best dancers in any of my classes. It was my dream from early on to become famous as an actor or a dancer. I would watch dancers on TV or on stage and wish to be like them.

As a young girl, I had lots of thoughts that would swim around in my head. I was often quiet, but inside my thoughts were loud. Before I ever tried alcohol or other drugs I was constantly searching for ways to get out of my head, away from self-judgment. So dancing for me became an escape. Theater became an escape. My imagination became an escape. For a while, these forms worked for me.

But then I became a teenager.[15]

Angela

She begins her story as a middle school student:

My name is Angela. I was born at Saint Joe's Hospital 17 years ago. I have lived in my small town all of my life. I have a mom and dad and brother. I also have a dog and a bird. My early home life was filled with good friends, ballet, homework, and fancy dresses. Everyone who surrounded me made me feel like a princess. I was very shy. I would cry when I would go sit on Santa's lap during Christmas time. I was always showered with presents and was always grandma's favorite.

When I was in 8th grade, the summer going into freshman year, my mom and dad separated and my mom, brother, and I moved to the city. They are now in the process of getting a divorce. In grade school I got As and Bs until 8th grade when my grades started to drop to Cs and Ds. Currently in high school, freshman year, I got Bs and Cs. I hate school and hate going. I hate the big classes and wish I could have smaller ones. I feel that homework should not be given because 7 hours is enough and that school work should be left in school. I know school is necessary to be successful in life but I just hate having to go for such a long day. My future plans include graduating and going to college. I'm not sure what I want to be when I grow up yet.[16]

Bonnie, Angela's mom shares in an interview, "Before high school, Angela was a part of the popular group. She was very happy and active, participating in lots of dance classes. Drugs seemed the furthest thing from her mind." *Once, when Angela and her mom (Bonnie) were picking out a movie to rent, Angela commented on someone at the store that she knew, saying,* "She is such a druggie. I can't understand why she'd do that."[17]

Arturo

He begins his story as an elementary student:

When I was in elementary school I had a gym teacher who was also a bus driver for the school. His big thing was saying no to drugs. The big phrase at the time was "Just say no," which in retrospect, worked for younger kids. I didn't need any explanation why I should "just say no." I just did. My gym teacher used to bring in pictures of people that had their jaws cut out because of chewing tobacco, etc. It was horrifying so I decided I would never use anything.[18]

Closing This Chapter

You know what you know now, based on your past experiences, which now includes what you've just read. You've learned about the brain and how it works. You've learned how portions of the brain are developed more than others when you are a teen. You've heard from professional people and resources about using substances, and you've read about real-life people. People who are or were teens, just like you in some ways. As you know, one of the best ways to learn is to keep asking questions.

At the end of each chapter, you might take time to jot down questions and thoughts that you have. Make sure that you seek out the answers to these questions and that you honor the thoughts you took the time to write down.

The next chapter deals with the substance path. It all begins when someone says yes.

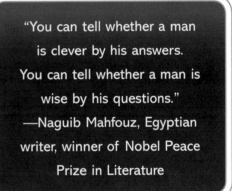

"You can tell whether a man is clever by his answers. You can tell whether a man is wise by his questions."
—Naguib Mahfouz, Egyptian writer, winner of Nobel Peace Prize in Literature

Notes

1. NIDA, "Drugs, Brains, and Behavior: The Science of Addiction," http://www.drugabuse.gov/publications/science-addiction/drug-abuse-addiction (accessed December 2012).
2. NIDA, "Drugs and the Brain," www.drugabuse.gov/publications/science-addiction/drugs-brain, updated August 2010 (accessed spring 2012).
3. Annenberg Lerner, "Neurotransmitters and Receptors," www.learner.org/courses/biology/textbook/neuro/neuro_7.html (accessed fall 2012).
4. NIDA, "Drugs and the Brain."
5. Pastor Janis Kinens, Advent Lutheran Church, interview with author, 2012.
6. Donna Bestor Krieger, former coordinator of the Alliance for a Drug-Free Wisconsin established by Governor Tommy Thompson, Attorney General Don Hanaway, and State Superintendent of Schools Herbert Grover, interview with author, 2012.
7. Lily was an eighth grader at the time of her written contribution, spring 2012.
8. Lon was a middle school student at the time of his first written contribution, spring 2012.

9. Brian was a middle school student at the time of his first written contribution, spring 2012.
10. Carol was an adult at the time of her written contribution, winter 2012.
11. Tim was an adult at the time of his written interview, winter 2012.
12. Brady was beyond high school at the time of his interview and written contribution, spring 2012.
13. Kyle was beyond high school at the time of his interview and written contribution, spring 2012.
14. Princess Peach was beyond high school at the time of her interview and written contribution, spring 2012.
15. Jessica was in her twenties at the time of her phone interview and written contribution, summer 2012.
16. Angela's story was received from an interview with her mom and from Angela's own writing, summer 2012.
17. Bonnie was interviewed in the summer of 2012.
18. Arturo provided a written interview midyear 2012.

EXPERIMENTING WITH SUBSTANCES

"When you are content to be simply yourself and don't compare or compete, everyone will respect you."—Lau Tzu, Tao Te China, father of Taoism

In this chapter we will discuss that "first use" of a substance by a teen. We'll chat more about the development of the teen brain and the effects of substances on the brain, and we'll hear from our teen friends as they tell their stories of their first uses.

Many youth find themselves confronted with the "choice" to try cigarettes, alcohol, or other drugs for the first time when they become a teenager, often between the ages of ten and twenty years old. The question becomes, Why do teens try drugs or alcohol, even when they've heard it isn't good for them and it is illegal? Many of the same teens who try substances are the ones who, at a younger age, promised themselves they would never choose to say yes. So what happens?

Why Try?

Pastor Janis Kinens comments on what factors he believes contribute to the first time a teen tries a substance: "I would think primarily curiosity . . . perhaps also a desire for affirmation and acceptance."[1]

Did you know?

"A new report finds that 76 percent of high school students have used tobacco, alcohol, marijuana, and other drugs, and one-fifth of them may be addicted."—Sharon Tanenbaum[2]

Janet Osherow, a coordinator of Family Services in Maryland, says, "Most of the kids just try it because that's what their friends are doing, it is a coping mechanism. For some they see their parents doing it."[3]

The former coordinator of the Alliance for Drug-Free Wisconsin, Donna Bestor Krieger, says,

> I don't think those that eventually experiment plan on using, rather, they reach a time in their lives when the opportunity is there, their friends are ready to experiment, and off they go. Many do not realize they are opening a Pandora's Box—something they may not be able to control. Some teens think using is something they will not do. However, as more and more of their friends join the "party group," they feel left out. They have a need to fit in and want to retain their friends. So they go along with the group. Opportunity plays a large factor in the first time a teen tries a substance, it is much easier for teens to experiment. If parents are closely involved, it is more difficult and the teen may not want to betray the trust the parents have in them.[4]

Ryan Byrne, MD, says,

> While this may seem simplistic, the best way to avoid substance use is to avoid situations in which you may be pressured to use substances. Adolescence is a time in which teenagers are trying to discover their identity and their peer group. Therefore, developmentally, it is difficult for teenagers to resist peer pressure. The best thing teens can do is pursue activities that are positive influences. These activities include sports, school clubs, and volunteering organizations. Another way to do this is to maintain a core group of friends who will back you up. If you are going somewhere new or are going to be with newer friends who may use, go with a friend who has agreed with you not to use substances.[5]

Why Are Teens *So* Important to Teens?

Remember when you read about the idea that teens begin to care more about what their friends think than their parents? Let's explore the concept of teens being guided by teens and how it may be a contributing factor to the trend of young people to turn away from their parents.

In, *Hold On to Your Kids: Why Parents Need to Matter More Than Peers*, the authors explain a concept called "peer-oriented teens."[6] "Peer-oriented children look to their peers, not to adults, to get their bearings and for their cues on how

Do your friends sometimes seem to matter more to you than your parents?

to be, how to see themselves, on what values to pursue."[7] So the idea is that if you replace your parents with your peers as your "north" (imagine a compass), then parents become south.[8] So what your friends say sounds good and cool and what your parents believe and say, well . . . doesn't. Do you find yourself thinking your parents are clueless and uncool? Do you have a hard time spending time with them, let alone opening up and talking with them?

According to the authors of *Hold On to Your Kids: Why Parents Need to Matter More Than Peers*, "Children cannot be oriented to both adults and other children simultaneously. One cannot follow two sets of conflicting directions at the same time. The child's brain must automatically choose between parental values and peer values, parental guidance and peer guidance, parental culture and peer culture whenever the two would appear to be in conflict."[9]

While it is healthy, as you mature, to begin to develop a more independent relationship from parents, peers relying on other kids the same age does not allow for natural maturity to develop. Instead, teens are encouraged to take their cues from each other.

How is your relationship with your friends versus your parents?

- How do you feel around your parents? Do you find yourself wanting to be with your family less and less and spend more time with your peers, almost to the point that it makes you uncomfortable if you have to be away from them for any extended length of time?
- Do you feel nervous if you have to miss something with your friends, almost like you are being left out and might not get back in?
- Are you almost desperate to be with your friends? Do you find it frustrating when your parents want you to spend time with your family?
- Do you look to your peers for advice about other friends, boy- and girlfriends, school, and family issues?
- Do you find yourself in constant connection with your friends, never taking time for yourself?
- Do you see yourself as your peers see you, and is that a truly accurate depiction of yourself?
- Do you value your own opinions more than your peers', or are you constantly working to be similar to your friends?

This way of looking to your peers may seem natural, and you might even think that it has always been this way, that teens act and dress like each other, that they care so much about what each other thinks, so why shouldn't you. You are all seeking approval from each other. This isn't unique to the teen population; in fact, there is a deep need for humans to feel included and loved at all stages in life. You might feel it is healthy. But what isn't always realized is that as much as you all love being with your friends, your friends aren't grown up either. Teens are facing many pressures as we discussed earlier. As lost as one teen might feel, when she turns to her friend, that teen may feel just as lost. Yet they try to guide each other, each needing something the other can't provide.

This can lead to even more distress, as pointed out in, *Hold On to Your Kids: Why Parents Need to Matter More Than Peers*: "What children fear more than anything, including physical harm, is getting lost. To them, being lost means losing contact with their compass point. Orienting voids, situations where we find

> ## ! A Different Take on "Choice"
>
> Remember when we talked about your brain development as a teen? Remember how that can affect decision making? From the book *In the Realm of Hungry Ghosts: Close Encounters with Addiction*, Dr. Gabor Maté says, "I hope it's clear, however, that in the real world choice, will, and responsibility are not absolute and unambiguous concepts. People choose, decide, and act in a context—and to a large degree that context is determined by how their brains function. The brain itself also develops in the real world and is influenced by conditions over which the individual, as a young child, had no choice whatsoever."[10]

nothing or no one to orient by, are absolutely intolerable to the human brain. Even adults who are relatively self-orienting can feel a bit lost when not in contact with the person in their lives who functions as their working compass point."[11]

So what does this mean to you? It means that teens like you will, at times, find themselves doing whatever it takes to fit in. Do you agree with this? Have you ever experienced this? And how do you think this affects the choice of using substances?

Some believe that teens who rely on other teens will do whatever it takes to avoid feelings of pain. These feelings can come in the form of insecurity, embarrassment, loneliness, and self-consciousness. So guess what? Enter substance use. It makes sense to some teens to turn to substances not only as a sure way to fit in with others who are using, but also, eventually, as a way to protect themselves from the pain of emotions. Substances can make teens feel less vulnerable.

Peers relying on each other is one factor in why teens become involved in substances. As you read in the last chapter, there are a variety of other reasons to add to the list of why a teen may say yes to trying.

The Teen's Brain

The National Institute on Drug Abuse (NIDA) states, "The brain continues to develop into adulthood and undergoes dramatic changes during adolescence."[12] Because the prefrontal cortex is still not fully developed, it puts you at increased risk for poor decision making. Let's face it. Who can bake a cake without all of the ingredients? Your "recipe" for solid decision making is a full and developed brain and that won't be done cooking for a while, teens. So be careful what you taste test.

The bottom line is, a teen tries a substance. Now what?

Thinking about How the Brain Thinks

The brain can be hard to understand (no matter how smart your brain is). After my interview with child and adolescent psychiatrist Dr. Ryan Byrne, he wrote,

Many teenagers are the size of adults and have completed the physical changes associated with adolescence. However, brain development continues into the early twenties for women and until close to thirty years old in men. This is important for two reasons. First, use of any substances that affect the brain's chemicals may alter this normal development of the brain. What has been shown is that the brains of people who use substances change to become "a machine" that simply tries to seek out more of the substance. Important things, like coping skills and interpersonal skills, are sacrificed for the substance. One concern is that, if teens turn to substances, they may never develop the coping and interpersonal skills that typically develop in adolescence.

Another important factor is that the last portion of the brain to develop is the frontal lobe of the brain. The frontal lobe is, essentially, "the brakes" of the brain. This is why teenagers, especially when confronted with peer pressure, make decisions that may not be in their best interest. It also causes teens to act in the moment instead of considering the future. Examples of this are teenagers who drive fast, get in fights, or spend a lot with their parent's credit card. A less serious example is a teenager who watches a movie instead of studying for a big test. Having a less developed frontal lobe also causes teenagers to think only of today and not consider what the results of their actions will be tomorrow, in two months, or in two years. The final part of this is that most teenagers are as smart, if not smarter, than older adults. However, in times of excitement or crisis, they don't have "brakes" on their brains. So, when teens face a lot of pressure to use substances, they may make a decision to use because they are not thinking of the future but only what seems right for the moment. It also, then, makes them more at risk for intoxication because the frontal lobe isn't there telling them to slow down.[13]

First Time Substance Use and the Teen Brain

So you have heard from doctors and researchers and experts on the reasons why a teen might say yes to trying substances. You have considered the development of the brain and learned about how peers rely on each other.

Drugs are chemicals, as you now know. They can interfere with the natural way the nerve cells send, receive, and process information by getting into the communication system. Remember when we talked about the brain and communication? Remember "It's all about communication"? Different drugs affect the brain differently; that is, drugs communicate differently with the brain. Some drugs act in a similar way that the natural neurotransmitters act and are able to "trick" the receptors into thinking they are the brain's neurotransmitters, a natural chemical. The drugs activate neurons. But because they don't act the same way a brain's neurotransmitters do, abnormal messages are sent through the brain. Two examples of this type of chemical reaction to the brain can be found with the use of marijuana and heroin. Drugs cause another reaction by nerve cells

Most often people get used to listening to the loudest sensation they hear.

releasing excessive amounts of natural neurotransmitters. This causes chaos in the communication channels through exaggerated messages to the brain. Examples are amphetamines and Ecstasy. You can imagine this by picturing the difference between a soft whisper and someone using a microphone. Most often people get used to listening to the loudest sensation they hear.

As mentioned in chapter 1, part of the limbic system is what is considered the "reward circuit of the brain." When pleasure is experienced, the brain normally releases the neurotransmitter dopamine (remember the warm chocolate chip cookie?), which signals the brain to remember it, to pay attention to it, to record it as *pleasure*. (This is why you might find yourself back in the kitchen with your hand in the cookie jar.) But drugs cause havoc on this intricate system, prompting large amounts of dopamine to flood the system. This is what is considered a "high" when taking drugs. When a teenager decides to use a drug, the feelings of pleasure are intense. Drugs of abuse affect the reward system. With this non-natural flood of neurotransmitters, *even on the first use*, the brain starts changing. Because the brain senses all of the dopamine (created because of the drug use), the neurons may begin to either make less dopamine or reduce the number of dopamine receptors. This whole process weakens the ability of the circuits that create pleasure. So the stuff that used to make you feel good (like that homemade cookie) might not cut it anymore. The brain now tells you that the chemical you took should be the goal from now on. Without it, you might begin to feel a low and you also might begin to equate drugs with pleasure and joy. And life without drugs becomes depressing. Then more drugs will be needed to bring dopamine levels up, which is called becoming "tolerant."

Our brains are set up to repeat behaviors and activities that keep us alive and happy. So those activities that bring pleasure, our brain wants to repeat, and the reward circuit is activated. It teaches the brain to do it again and then again, without even thinking about it. This same process happens with drug use.

Feelings with a First Use

Guilt, excitement, disappointment, fear, pressure . . . so many feelings can accompany a first try. Let's find out what happened in the stories by teens who found themselves facing "the choice."

Lily

Lily has not experimented or tried any substances as of the publishing of this book, and therefore, her story continues on but not in this book.

Lon

Sometimes I wonder . . .

Are all towns like mine? I feel like once I turned ten and into double digits, the place I live and people around me changed. I started hearing about drugs and alcohol from

"It's not the situation . . . it's your reaction to the situation."—Bob Conklin, teacher, speaker, author

peers. It wasn't until I was eleven when I was first introduced to it though. I was at a friend's house babysitting our younger siblings playing Barbies when she takes out a Mike's Hard Lemonade and asks me if I want one. In my family, drinking was something you just don't do. Some parents let their kids take sips, but my parents didn't believe in that, so of course I said no. I wasn't offered again 'til I was twelve and I was at the park with some friends. Some guys one year older had a bottle of vodka that they stole from their parents. All the people I was with gave in and drank, but I didn't. A few months later, all those people got caught. My parents told me how grateful they were of me for not doing it and not giving in. One of my friend's parents came up to my mom and said, "I don't know what you guys are doing, but I do know you're doing something right." I felt so proud because my parents had taught me how to make the right decisions, but also because they taught me how to stand up for myself.

I got offered a few more times that year but when I was thirteen was when I started getting offered drugs, weed, cigarettes, K2, and more. Sometimes I wouldn't even know what they were asking me to try and there would be times when I wouldn't even get invited because the people there knew I wouldn't give in. Yes it hurt. I felt alone because all my friends were doing things and going places that seemed cool. Most of my friends have given in a few times and so I always felt left out. They would ask me why I don't and I have to think about my future. I've read books like *Tweak* and I know how easily it is to get addicted.

There were many times when I wanted to finally say yes. To be included and to feel cool, but I would stop and think. I don't think I'm better than the people who use drugs or alcohol. I don't know if I'm smarter or I'm going to have a better future than them but I do know that I'm making the right choices, that will make the people around me proud, make me feel better about myself, and ultimately make me and my life the best it can be.

Well my good streak didn't last long. I could only take so much, before I gave in. I had become part of a group of girls that I considered my best friends. They were good kids and we had so much fun together. I was at a bonfire with all of them. I didn't know there was going to be drinking there, but soon enough, some girls pulled out a water bottle of vodka and started passing it around. I blocked everything out of my mind so I wouldn't worry, like, what could happen to me or if I'd get into trouble. I don't really know how many sips I had, but when I got home, I knew I was dead meat. I didn't feel good and I felt light-headed. My mom said she could smell the alcohol from down the driveway. I felt so awful that I had let my parents down, and lost their trust.

I don't know why I took that sip of alcohol, or those few chugs that followed. Maybe it was the fact that it was summer and I didn't have to worry about school. Or maybe because I felt grown up, just graduating middle school I didn't feel like a little kid anymore. But I think it's because I was with my closest friends. The people I wanted to spend every second with and I could trust them with my life. So if they could take a few sips and be fine, then why couldn't I?[14]

Brian

I don't know how it happened or really why it happened but my 8th grade year I tried alcohol. Something changed in my brain and I wasn't really scared anymore, in fact I was kind of curious. I still remember that day, we were all in my friend's basement and someone asked if we had ever tried it, we all replied with a "no." At this point I was thinking about all of the things my parents had told me, but I also thought that it was only one sip and it couldn't hurt me. So when it came my turn to take a sip I did it. It tasted horrible and my throat burned. But surprisingly enough I didn't die, and the world didn't stop. I had a couple more sips after that and I became the dreaded word what my parents called drunk. Waking up the next morning was not a fun experience, I didn't feel too good and I was really scared of my parents. At that point I didn't really want to do it again. I just always wanted to know what it was like so I was glad I found out. A couple weeks later word got about our night, and my mom and dad found out. I don't think I have ever cried that hard in my life before, I was not crying because I regretted doing it or I thought I was a bad person it was more disapproval from my parents, it was the worst thing in the world. We talked it all out and they of course forgave me and said they loved me.[15]

Carol

I started smoking in college, I was 18, a few months before I was turning 19. It was actually one of the first days I was there. A girl on my floor (who

I kind of knew) and I realized we were about the only people who weren't smoking so we decided to try it. It was fun and made us feel like we fit in better.[16]

Tim

I didn't go to parties where people drank. But the summer of my junior year I was in a basketball league and after we all ended up at a senior party. I took my first drink. It was a beer. I didn't feel peer pressure from others but I did want to fit in, and so I thought, what the hell. Once I drank, I felt like I was more outgoing and I could let loose and approach girls easier. That night I got drunk. My parents didn't find out. I didn't really feel bad about it, I thought it was fun.[17]

Brady

One of the scariest moments for me happened when I was a junior in high school. I didn't use pills really, only every once in a while. I would experiment with them. One day one of my friends came to school with some Ambien and some muscle relaxers. He gave me three Ambien and two muscle relaxers. I wasn't aware of what the actual muscle relaxers were. He said he got them from his parents (took them) when he gave them to me he told me to take them all. That's what he did. He was also bigger and had a higher tolerance. But I took them. They kicked in quick. I was seeing double of everything. By my next class it got worse. I was pale white. Luckily my best friend was in the class and he told me I looked like I was a ghost or dying or something. Luckily he snuck me out of class and then took me to the bathroom where I threw up. Then I went to lie down in the office. If it wasn't for my friend who knows what would have happened.[18]

Kyle

When I first tried drugs or alcohol it basically had put me in an entire different world. But it was a world I was very comfortable with, the way it made me feel, made me want to be high and or drunk more often. It made it seem like all the pain and discomfort was gone. I felt relieved and liked that a lot. It was me and a couple of my friends were partying one night. Give or take I was around 14 or 15 years old. We had drugs and alcohol pretty much you named it we had it. Seeing all of it made me think to my-self about my goal for life. Then the thought of if I don't do it what will my friends think of me. I didn't want to be singled out so I drank and did a lot of drugs. Mind you this was the first time doing it and was my first time seeing drugs and alcohol. Later I found myself passed out on the couch to awake and seeing all the rest of the people all spread out still asleep. As I laid there I tried my very hardest to try to remember how the rest of the night went. But for some reason I just couldn't. Then I said to myself must have been that good. Afterwards I felt a slight headache coming on. I then learned for this to be what's called a hangover. I felt like total crap. I was afraid my parents would notice but thankfully they never suspected anything out of the ordinary. I wanted to do it all over. I felt I had control to basically put myself to a limit.[19]

Princess Peach

I first tried my very first mood altering chemical "drug" when I was in eighth grade; I was thirteen years old then. It was our eighth grade gradu-ation before we entered high school. The very last day of school, before summer was here, I was with my childhood friend and another peer of mine I went to school with. I was "peer pressured" into it. I never really said yes to using the substance. The substance was marijuana. We were at a local campsite type setting where immigrants would come from other states and stay for usually the summer. We were with two older gentlemen that the other girl had known and I think my friend was dating. They of-fered us a joint and my peers had all smoked marijuana before but I had not. I was then pressured into it. I remember the older guys blowing the smoke in my mouth to get high and then I was brave enough to pick up the joint and put it to my lips and smoke it as my peers were. After we were done, I felt light-headed and like I was not myself. I felt relaxed and like I was floating in thin air. My body went through the typical effects mari-juana makes you feel, mellowed out, hungry "the munchies," and sleepy.

I felt about the decision afterwards, as if I had a guilty conscience be-cause I knew wrong from right then. I knew I was not going to die from smoking marijuana and knew it was a lot safer drug than other things; that I guess led my mind to believe I could get away with it and use it. I felt like I let myself down and was not living up to my parents' expectations of me. I think mainly I felt disappointed I did something I always avoided prior to that day. I never wanted to consider myself a "pot head," a person that sat home all day, ate potato chips. I never wanted to be the statistic of a nonproductive member of society because they have no drive or motivation in life due to the marijuana.[20]

Jessica

The first time I ever used alcohol to the point I was drunk was at a party. I was thirteen. My parents were actually there with me. Though I had always been taught not to use, watching movies, going to musicals, even watching TV, it always seemed that drinking and drugs were glamorized within the story lines, so trying for the first time didn't seem like that big of a deal to me. So I snuck off and drank with the older kids who offered it to me. I wanted to be like them. There wasn't peer pressure, but somehow it was definitely permission. Permission to join the higher rank.

That first drunk was like magic. I was relieved from the thoughts in my head of self-judgment, and there was no work involved for me. The alcohol did the work for me. So it was magical and it made me dizzy. When I was driving home from that party, with my parents in the front seat and me in the back, I remember feeling guilty about what I had just done but then when they didn't say anything—when they didn't catch me, I got another rush because I got away with it.[21]

Angela

Bonnie, Angela's mom, shares, "In eighth grade an incident occurred which left Angela ostracized from her group of friends. She did not reach out to adults to share this until the end of the year. By then, her grades slipped to Cs and Ds. Moving on to freshman year and then becoming a sophomore, Angela got her first job. She felt more confident about herself and with that, she became much more curious with older kids, spending more time with them and their families. She began to be more open with me about topics and found these older kids interesting, even those who were using drugs. This brought down the barriers she once had about drug use." *It was a girl who Angela worked with that introduced her to pot the first time. Her mom noticed that she had used, but Angela at the time denied it. She knew it would disappoint her mom.*[22]

Arturo

As I got into middle school I worried more about making friends and what other people thought of me. I got mixed up with kids that were smoking cigarettes because of class schedule and my bus routes. In the town I lived in the bus routes are long so you have a lot of time to talk and plan trouble making. I tried my first cigarette. Disgusting. It makes me sick still and I went on later to smoke a pack a day. I got dizzy and almost threw up. I was not amused so I never did it again. At that age anyway. A few months later I was walking on the bike path in town and a kid we were with had pot. He offered us so the girls I was with and I smoked. I was the only one smoking for the first time. I did not get high. But I did cough a lung up. I also hated that and regretted it deeply. I knew my parents would be ashamed of me if they found out so I promised myself that I would quit and also stop hanging out with those kids. We moved to this town the next year halfway through eighth grade. I had an easy time making friends. I was skate boarding and doing all the things 8th graders do.[23]

Closing This Chapter

As you move on to the next chapter, ask yourself some questions. Can you relate to any of the teens' thoughts on feeling included, excluded? Even if your friends don't pressure you, do you feel a sense of pressure that you put on yourself? Have you ever pressured someone else to try a substance? If so, how did that make you feel when he or she said yes, or said no? Why do you think you felt that way?

"Be yourself, not your idea of what you think somebody else's idea of yourself should be."
—Henry David Thoreau, American author, poet, and philosopher

Trying substances for the first time might seem like a natural experiment for a teen to experience. Read on to see what the first time try can lead to.

Notes

1. Pastor Janis Kinens, Advent Lutheran Church, interview with author, 2012.
2. Sharon Tanenbaum , "13 Sobering Facts about Teen Substance Abuse," Everyday Health, last updated, June 29, 2011, www.everydayhealth.com/kids-health-pictures/13-sobering-facts -about-teen-substance-abuse.aspx#/slide-1.
3. Janet Osherow, LICSW-Family Services Coordinator, Maryland, contributed in 2012.
4. Donna Bestor Krieger, former coordinator of the Alliance for a Drug-Free Wisconsin established by Governor Tommy Thompson, Attorney General Don Hanaway, and State Superintendent of Schools Herbert Grover, contributed in 2012.
5. Ryan R. Byrne, MD, assistant professor at the Medical College of Wisconsin, child and adolescent psychiatrist at Children's Hospital of Wisconsin, contributed in 2012.

6. Gordon Neufeld and Gabor Maté, *Hold On to Your Kids: Why Parents Need to Matter More Than Peers* (New York: Ballentine Books, 2006).

7. Neufeld and Maté, *Hold On to Your Kids*, 271.

8. Neufeld and Maté, *Hold On to Your Kids*, 8

9. Neufeld and Maté, *Hold On to Your Kids*, 8

10. Gabor Maté, *In the Realm of Hungry Ghosts: Close Encounters with Addiction* (Berkeley, CA: North Atlantic, 2010), 182.

11. Neufeld and Maté, *Hold On to Your Kids*, 19

12. NIDA, "Drugs, Brains, and Behavior: The Science of Addiction," http://www.drugabuse.gov/publications/science-addiction/drug-abuse-addiction (accessed December 2012).

13. Byrne, contribution.

14. Lon was a teenager at the time of his written contribution, spring 2012.

15. Brian was in high school at the time of his written contribution, 2012.

16. Carol was an adult at the time of her written contribution, fall 2012.

17. Tim was in his forties at the time of his written contribution, 2012.

18. Brady was beyond high school at the time of his written contribution, 2012.

19. Kyle was beyond high school at the time of his written contribution, 2012.

20. Princess Peach was beyond high school at the time of her written contribution, 2012.

21. Jessica was in her twenties at the time of her phone interview, 2012.

22. Bonnie shared Angela's story and her writing in an in-person interview, 2012.

23. Arturo shared his story through a written contribution, 2012.

INCREASED SUBSTANCE USE/ PREVENTION OF ADDICTION

"Just be yourself, there is no one better."
—*Taylor Swift, American singer-songwriter*

The experimental phase is over, yet some teens find themselves continuing to use. Why? What are the reasons teens continue to use long after that experimentation phase has ended?

In this chapter you will read about the continued use, what plays into the decisions and actions, and how the brain is affected, and you will hear from teenagers on what it was like for them.

Parents and Peers and What Keeps Teens Using

Obviously, having a strong and loving relationship with a parent can help make children feel secure and aid teens when it comes to making decisions, which you already know. But when teens rely on their friends for the needs they should be getting met by a parent, it is bound to create a sense of feeling self-conscious, vulnerable, and insecure because they are relying on friends who are feeling self-conscious, vulnerable, and insecure. This is often one of the reasons that leads teens to continue using substances past the experimental stage. Taking substances, for some teens, feels safe and feels good.

According to Judith Ford, a psychotherapist I interviewed for this book, additional factors that keep kids using include the following:

- Preexisting depression and/or anxiety
- Lack of friends that don't use
- Low self-esteem
- The reward centers of the brain that get activated by drugs—highly reinforcing, leading to cravings
- Seeking relief from negative physical and emotional aftermath of using, like guilt, fatigue, impaired concentration, and so on
- Inability to manage affect (never learned how to regulate own feelings—like what do you do when you're sad, no language for what is happening to them, don't know how to analyze or express feelings or how to identify them just in their own minds)
- Nothing in their lives can match the good feelings they get from being high—like lack of shyness, feeling "cool," a sense of power
- Lack of success in other areas
- Feeling alone, that no one understands them
- Social anxiety[1]

"Did you ever see an unhappy horse? Did you ever see a bird that had the blues? One reason why birds and horses are not unhappy is because they are not trying to impress other birds and horses."—Dale Carnegie, lecturer, writer, and developer of self-improvement courses

---

What Happens to the Brain with Continued Substance Use?

As the brain is maturing, it goes through what some call the "use it or lose it" principle. The brain is a communication network (there's that term again) that is complex, with billions of nerve cells, or "neurons." These networks of neurons transfer messages to and from the brain, the spinal column, and the peripheral nervous system. Controlling everything we feel, do, and think means that the neural connections, or synapses, that get used are retained, and those that aren't, are pruned, or lost. So the bottom line is that if you spend your time watching TV, you are hardwiring your brain for this activity. If you spend your time playing a musical instrument, you are hardwiring your brain for that activity. Which do you think helps your brain to grow more? Now consider what happens when your activity of choice is taking drugs or alcohol?

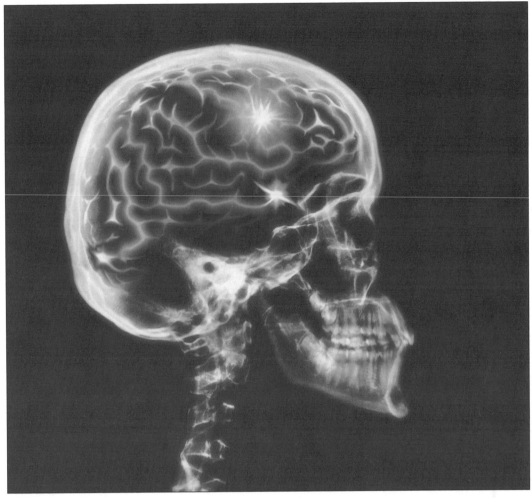

It's common knowledge that the brain is considered a control center of the body.

It's common knowledge that the brain is considered a control center of the body. It has many parts that work together to help the body function. Drugs can actually alter the way the brain functions. These alterations are a contributing factor leading to addiction or substance abuse disorders.

So if drug use changes brains, and teen brains aren't yet fully developed, it makes sense that using drugs when you are younger (a teen) may increase your chances of more serious drug use or becoming addicted. It seems obvious, but it is important to realize that the time when research says substance use increases (teen years) is also the time that is risky for more serious outcomes from that use. And there's more. Research suggests that at times of transition, drug abuse increases for teens, times like switching schools, your family structure shifting, a death or a loss. So, although it is obvious that substances are dangerous for anyone, teens have a lot of reasons to stay clear of them.

"A friend is someone who gives you total freedom to be yourself—and especially to feel, or not feel. Whatever you happen to be feeling at any moment is fine with them. That's what real love amounts to—letting a person be what he really is."—Jim Morrison, American singer-songwriter and poet

Does Continued Use Lead to Addiction?

Can addiction be prevented? If prevention was simple, there wouldn't be books being written, movies being filmed, and teens dying of addiction every day. No one wants to be addicted. There are teens who make it through the years between middle school and high school and move on to lead substance-free lives. But then there are the countless others who end up with substance abuse disorders. What is it that makes one teen become addicted and another not?

Who Will Become Addicted?

There are many risk factors that can lead a person to become addicted, and at this point in time, no one can definitely determine exactly when one person's use would change from using to becoming a disorder. We do know that each use affects the brain, making changes that move it toward an unhealthy state that could lead to addiction.

There is one sure way to ensure that addiction to substances never happens—never ingest substances. While this may seem obvious and simple, so many people who I interviewed wished that they hadn't taken the risk.

Not taking substances may seem like an obvious choice, but for teens under pressure with other risk factors, it isn't always so easy. The word *choice*, too, is one that holds a heavy burden. Most adults say, "Oh, just make the right choice." "Oh, you made the wrong choice." But sometimes it is more complicated because teens aren't always equipped with the tools to make these decisions easily. That's why, instead of letting this be an excuse, I've provided some alternatives so that teens aren't faced with these decisions. Each of the following suggestions includes actions that can be taken, but within each action must be intention as well as understanding.

- Evaluate your relationships with adults. Have you lost the connection with them? Do you think you have turned away from them? Can you find an adult who you can trust and who will offer you unconditional love to help you as you mature into an adult? Can you allow this adult to be your guide, so that you are nurtured by someone with wisdom and maturity?

- Consider the pros and cons of using substances. Write them down. Differentiate feelings from reality. Understand that your actions don't have to follow your feelings, so just because you are feeling lonely and worried you won't fit in, it doesn't mean you have to use a substance to lessen those feelings. Listen to your intuition but be wary of feelings of insecurity and the desire to fit in at all costs.
- Don't put yourself in a situation where you have to make a choice under pressure. Stay away from the peers who might pressure you.

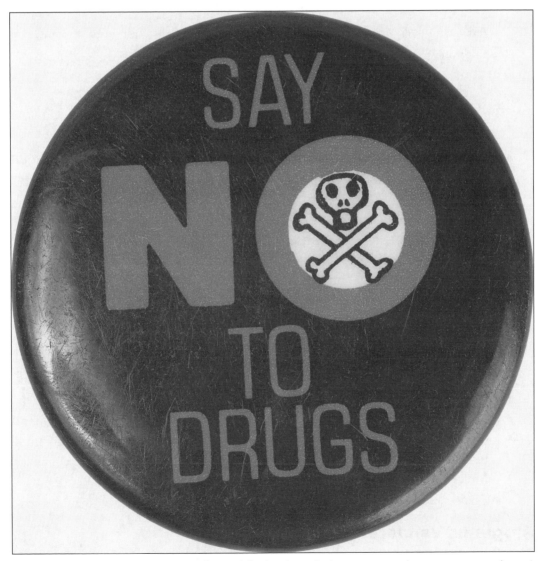

There is one sure way to ensure that addiction to substances never happens—never ingest substances.

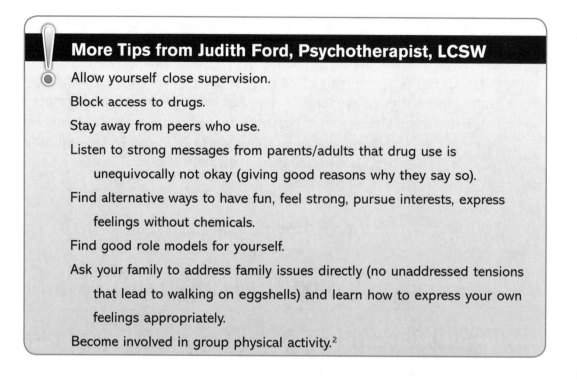

More Tips from Judith Ford, Psychotherapist, LCSW

Allow yourself close supervision.

Block access to drugs.

Stay away from peers who use.

Listen to strong messages from parents/adults that drug use is unequivocally not okay (giving good reasons why they say so).

Find alternative ways to have fun, feel strong, pursue interests, express feelings without chemicals.

Find good role models for yourself.

Ask your family to address family issues directly (no unaddressed tensions that lead to walking on eggshells) and learn how to express your own feelings appropriately.

Become involved in group physical activity.[2]

- Finish reading this book so that you can equip yourself with information and ideas to establish your own stable sense of where you stand on this issue.
- Become involved in something that you feel good about and that surrounds you with people who don't use.
- Become involved in something that helps feed your creativity, like drawing, painting, acting, singing, dancing, or writing.
- Stay close with your family members. If they encourage time spent together, do it.
- Realize your peers aren't your guides. Listen to your own intuition.
- Count your blessings—consider all that you have going for you, and why you wouldn't want to lose it.
- Consider getting to know yourself. Sometimes this helps by becoming involved in a religion, pursuing spirituality, or meditating so that you spend quiet time, learning to enjoy your own presence and feeling comfortable being alone.
- Make some goals for your future.

Programs Validated by Science

Science-validated programs are designed to help prevent drug addiction in youth. They have been designed based on current knowledge; they have been tested and

> ## Drug Prevention Programs
>
> According to the National Institute on Drug Abuse, "These prevention programs work to boost protective factors and eliminate or reduce risk factors for drug use. The programs are designed for various ages and can be designed for individual or group settings, such as the school and home. There are three types of programs:
>
> - Universal programs address risk and protective factors common to all children in a given setting, such as a school or community.
> - Selective programs target groups of children and teens who have factors that further increase their risk of drug abuse.
> - Indicated programs are designed for youth who have already begun abusing drugs."[3]

have shown to have positive results. These programs can lower the early use of alcohol, illicit drugs, and tobacco. NIDA is a resource for these programs.[4]

"I can always stop when I want to." Have you heard these words before? Have you thought them yourself, or has your friend said them, or your brother or sister? These are the words that run through the thoughts of many teens who are using substances. See if any of the following thoughts have come and gone through your mind:

Everyone else is doing it.
They don't have a problem. Why would I develop one?
No one ever got hurt with one try.
This little amount can't make me addicted.
I feel so much better. Stronger. Funnier . . . when I use . . .

And so the cycle continues. A person begins using—drinking or trying drugs—perhaps in a social setting. The frequency increases as perhaps the riskiness of using does as well. People continue to use because it makes them feel good or makes them not feel bad. Oftentimes teens move from trying a beer or other type of alcohol to marijuana, and then they try a more potent drug. The experimentations, as they are thought of, continue to escalate. How would you know if you are just a casual user or if you are developing a problem? The scary thing is that while all use affects your mind and body, becoming addicted can severely impact your life and the lives of those around you, and it is often very hard for someone who is using to know he or she has crossed the line from using to abusing. We will explore the warning signs and symptoms in the next chapter. But first . . .

Think about what makes you happy, excited, peaceful, joyful. Close your eyes, and envision

the first snowfall with big white flakes.
knowing every answer on a test.
winning the game.
sledding down a hill, fast.
water skiing in cool water on a hot day.
getting out of a lake, feeling cold, and letting the warm sun begin to dry you.
the tug of a fish on the end of your pole.
waking up and realizing it's Saturday and there's no school, so you can fall
   back to sleep.
thunderstorms.
your birthday morning.
sitting in the woods.
warm rain, hot blacktop, squishy worms.
your favorite song.

Now imagine that nothing, nothing from this list, nothing from your own list, nothing can give you the high it used to, before drugs began messing with your brain. Your brain will change if you take drugs and alcohol. That is a fact. In time, the only highs you will be able to attain will be from chemical substances. It's true. Let's hear from firsthand experiences.

Personal Stories

Lily's contribution appears in chapter 1 and Lon's story appears in chapters 1 and 2. At the time this book was being published, neither had any more to share on the topic.

Brian

I then entered high school, everyone thinks it's like the end of the world if you don't drink, and it's not. After my 8th grade experience I never really tried it again, sure a few sips here and there. But I realized that it's not worth all the horrible things that can happen to you such as drunk driving, sex, suspended from sports, and a lot of other things that aren't worth one wild night. There are so many other things that you can do besides drinking and drugs. I am lucky that I could experiment with alcohol and come out just fine. Some people don't and they become alcoholics. I know a lot of people who it hasn't been just that one time experimenting and it led them down a horrible path. Now I'm not saying that it isn't hard. A lot of parties I go to people are doing it all around me, and I do get asked frequently. But high school isn't as bad as all the movies say it is. People don't make you do anything you don't want to do if you just say no. I don't know if my first encounter with alcohol was a bad thing or a good thing. But I'm glad I can say no now and feel good about it.

[*Brian's story continues one year later.*] Getting arrested was like a nightmare that I thought would never happen to me. I only saw it in movies and TV shows. None of my family or friends has ever been arrested and I sure never thought it would ever happen to me. Then everything changed for me. On the way to a soccer game, me and my friends were invited to a senior's house. When we got there everyone was drinking. Someone asked me if I wanted a shot. I thought about my choices and decided since I was not driving and it was only one shot it would be okay. I took the shot and continued talking to my friends. We then walked to the game and I went and stood by my friends. We were winning the game and I was really excited. I was not worried about getting in trouble at all. My friends and I decided to go get some food. We walked behind the stands and started heading towards the food stand. We got stopped by a cop and he asked if we had been drinking; I only had one shot so I lied and said no. He pulled out a breathalyzer and told me to blow into it. I did as I was told and he told me I lied and had been drinking and forced me to sit down. I looked up and saw my principals and friends' parents looking down at me, looks of disappointment and disapproval. I started crying not thinking that this was real life. The police pulled us up and handcuffed me in front of the entire soccer team, principals, teachers, and pretty much the entire city. They walked me over to the police cars and had me stand against the cars as if I were a criminal. Everyone was staring at me while I cried and was humiliated. They pushed me into the side of the cop car and drove away. We got to the station and they shoved me into locked rooms where I sat and cried. It looked just like the rooms in movies when the people are interrogated. I got mug shot and finger printed. Then I called my mom. It was a horrible call to have to make; I was both scared of her but also I felt like I used to when I was a little kid and I needed her. My dad came and picked me up with my little brother. I had to have a meeting with the vice principal, go to a community service class, and I was suspended for four days. It was horrible, humiliating. I guess what I've learned is that no matter how much I think drinking isn't dangerous, it is. Because in its own way, it hurt me. What I realize is it just isn't worth it. It is against the law. Even if someone doesn't think something will hurt you, you still have to follow the rules.[5]

Carol

It soon became a habit, something I did when studying, talking on the phone or to someone, drinking coffee or beer. There were many situations that seemed to be more fun or more tolerable when smoking. Almost everyone smoked at that time so it was a sort of common denominator among us all. There was no problem smoking in restaurants, bars, or the workplace. Or even while you were pregnant. So time went on and I kept smoking. Opinions as well as the knowledge about the safety of smoking has changed dramatically since then.[6]

Tim

By senior year we were drinking every night. By college I tried to quit drinking. But then I would have issues, like girlfriend issues, and then I would drink heavily again. Drinking numbed the problem for the night. Then the problem would seem worse. So during college I would get a keg and a few of us would finish it in a night. We didn't think about how much we were drinking. We would drink a lot before we even went out, with a big bottle of booze. When we were out I would go to bars or parties and drink more. It didn't seem like a problem. I didn't think anything of my drinking. The people I hung around with drank the same amount. I never did drugs because my sisters were into heavy drugs, like heroin. We had so much money that they could afford it. Bored kids, we had nothing but money. I went to a therapist with them when I was little, like 10 years old, and I remember not fully understanding but I was worried about them. I felt like I was being punished having to go there.[7]

Kyle

I wanted to do it [get drunk and high] all over. I felt I had control to basically put myself to a limit.[8]

Princess Peach

When we can stop we don't want to![9]

Jessica

So my parents and I would go to parties or have parties where the kids were always invited. We'd separate from the adults. I had a stash of vodka and whiskey that I hid in my room, and when friends would come over, we would drink. Each time we did this I experienced the effect of the alcohol with the rush of getting away with doing it without my parents knowing. Through all of this I never stopped dancing. Eventually, I started hanging around college kids because I was a good enough dancer to be in shows with them. They were into alcohol and marijuana. This was completely acceptable to me in my mind because they were living on their own. I was 15, and though young, they wouldn't discriminate because of my age. Joining in their substance use was a way for me to fit in, to break the ice. I was no longer sneaking vodka with my friends in my room—now I was with people who were older and not my peers. I wanted to keep up.[10]

Angela

Second semester of sophomore year Angela's grades began to drop again. Her mom took dance away from her letting her know that school had to come first. But then Angela started missing school. Her mom would drop her off and Angela would walk into school, only to leave shortly after. Often Angela would go back home to the empty house, bringing other kids with her. When her mom was at work, they would use drugs. It got to the point, the summer before junior year, where Angela wasn't allowed to have a key to her house.

Angela shared in her journal,

I have received three truancy tickets all during sophomore year. I was put on probation for one year during April for possession of Adderall [a medication that can be used for the treatment of ADHD and narcolepsy and contains amphetamine]. I have used drugs and alcohol. Freshman year I started drinking and smoking marijuana. Sophomore year I increased my smoking to every day, continued drinking, started using aderol every day for two months in the winter, then started using cocaine every day from

January to March, used mushrooms, a couple of times, abused opiate painkiller pills, tried salvia a couple times, and started smoking cigarettes. Then in June I tried LSD a couple times and ecstasy a couple times and continued drinking heavily.[11]

Arturo

In high school I had ok grades but school was less interesting to me than hanging out with my friends. At the end of freshman year a friend of mine asked me if I wanted to buy pot with him for a party we were going to. I felt like being adventurous so I said yes. My decision was simple because my basic philosophy was an atheistic one. We only live once. This was my basic philosophy regarding how I would lead my life all through high school. I felt that doing drugs was part of exploring the limits of my body and getting to know myself in a way. I looked at the experiences I had with different types of drugs like some people collect stamps. That was high school in a nutshell. The first three years of school anyway. Senior year I went to a boarding school. My parents sent me there to get away from the kids I was spending a lot of time with. I turned eighteen there. I was not ready to change. My friends had been experimenting with heroin while I was gone. My best friend overdosed badly at a friend's house. He survived but was never the same when I came back, he seemed like a shell. I was sure I would stay away from heroin altogether. . . . Weed was fulfilling me at the time. I met Angela [referring to the Angela in this book] through a friend of mine that lived in my neighborhood. We talked about music and she impressed me. After that day we spent a lot of time together. She was better to me than I deserved at that point in my life. One day I came over to her house after work and she had a freezer baggie half full of opiates she had taken from her dad's house. We took them every day for almost a month before it was empty.[12]

> "Don't you ever let a soul in the world tell you that you can't be exactly who you are."
> —Lady Gaga, songwriter, singer, dancer, actress, record producer, activist, fashion designer, philanthropist

Closing This Chapter

Moving from experimenting to using more to abusing is a slippery slope. It's tough to assess where someone is on the spectrum. It's all to be taken pretty seriously, because every sip, smoke, pill, or powder taken will affect your mind, body, and overall self. If you know of someone who you feel is in danger or you yourself think you have a problem, it is really important you find an adult you can trust and share. Right now.

Notes

1. Judith Ford, psychotherapist, LCSW, interview with author and written contribution, 2012.
2. Ford, interview and written contribution.
3. NIDA, "Drugs, Brains, and Behavior: The Science of Addiction," http://www.drugabuse.gov/publications/science-addiction/preventing-drug-abuse-best-strategy (accessed 2012).
4. NIDA, "Drugs, Brains, and Behavior."
5. Brian contributed as a teenager, 2012.
6. Carol was an adult at the time of her written contribution, 2012.
7. Tim was an adult at the time of his written contribution, 2012.
8. Kyle was out of high school at the time of his contribution, 2012.
9. Princess Peach was out of high school at the time of her written contribution, 2012.
10. Jessica was in her twenties at the time of her phone interview and written contribution, 2012.
11. Angela's mom shared Angela's story and her writing in 2012.
12. Arturo shared his story in a written letter in 2012.

ADDICTION

"*Never bend your head. Always hold it high. Look the world straight in the face.*"
—*Helen Keller, American author, political activist, and lecturer*
who lost her sight and her hearing as a child

Let's Talk

The process of using substances can lead to addiction. In this chapter, you will read about addiction, the signs and symptoms, and you will explore what happens to the brain. You will hear from our teen writers.

What Is Addiction?

According to Gabor Maté, MD, author of the book *In the Realm of Hungry Ghosts: Close Encounters with Addiction*, "Addiction is any repeated behavior, substance-related or not, in which a person feels compelled to persist, regardless of its negative impact on his life and the lives of others. Addiction involves:

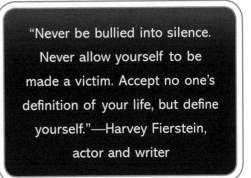

"Never be bullied into silence. Never allow yourself to be made a victim. Accept no one's definition of your life, but define yourself."—Harvey Fierstein, actor and writer

1. compulsive engagement with the behavior, a preoccupation with it;
2. impaired control over the behavior;
3. persistence or relapse despite evidence of harm; and
4. dissatisfaction, irritability, or intense craving when the object—be it a drug, activity, or other goal—is not immediately available."[1]

So one might wonder if a person experiments with substances, and then continues to use, can't he or she simply stop when he or she wants, before addiction sets in? There are many layers to the subject of addiction that relates to the brain

What It Felt Like

"When I would start to run out of my pills, I would start to get nervous, because I knew I'd go through withdrawals. And even though I wasn't getting a buzz anymore, I needed the pills just to maintain. That feeling is the worst. You feel crawling up your spine, you can't stop moving, everything aches, every fiber of your body aches, you can't stop moving even if you have to go to the bathroom, you can't stop. And it gets worse as the days go on. You start looking all around your room for just one pill you could find, one more to get you through. There is a footprint in your brain from when you were using, if you go through withdrawals and then start out again, the cravings will go back to what you had, even if you think you can control it. You can't. The worst of it is the feeling of impending doom. Everything is crashing down on you. You think about everything; you feel so bad about spending money, not having a job, or skipping a day of work, everything you were blocking out is just there all of a sudden. It is mental anguish. Anxiety. Nothing is worse than anxiety. I didn't have enough energy to even walk up the stairs. My heart rate would beat super-fast. You can't sleep, you just roll around in your bed and having no sleep just adds to it. You can't eat; you know you have to so you might get down a candy bar. It was too hard to keep it up; every day I would wake up and chase it. That's what I spent my time doing. It becomes everything you're doing; it takes up all of your time. It consumes your every moment."—Tristessa, an addicted teen[2]

and the body. While it seems that all it would take is willpower to stop using, as you probably already realize, it is more complicated than that. When drugs begin to make changes in the brain, a teen's power of self-control is hampered. Images that were taken of brains that were addicted to substances shows physical changes in the parts of the brain that are important for behavior control.

What Happens to the Brain with Addiction?

As you know now, the limbic system is at work when you feel natural pleasures, like when you do well on a test or someone says something nice to you. These

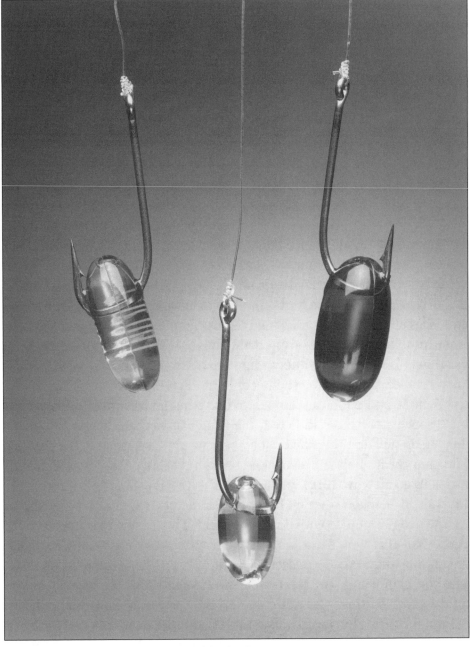

What happens to the brain with addiction?

natural feelings are important for survival. Just like your body tells you to eat when you are hungry, your brain tells you to be "hungry" for those good feelings so that you seek them out.

When someone uses a substance the first time, she or he may have intense feelings of pleasure. Dopamine is carrying the message in the activated reward circuitry. This is just one of the effects of substance use. You might also react physically to the toxins by feeling like throwing up, getting a headache, feeling dizzy, and so on.

Because of this flood of neurotransmitters, which is unnaturally caused by the substances, the brain begins to change. Neurons either make less dopamine or cut back on the number of dopamine receptors because they sense that there is more than enough dopamine from the effects of the substance use. Some of the neurons may also die because of the toxicity of the drugs.

Remember how dopamine carries the message in the activated reward circuitry? When the drugs begin to affect the brain and dopamine is cut back, its ability to activate the circuits to cause pleasure are then weakened. After the intense rush of pleasure, the person now feels depressed, lifeless, and dull. A person may feel joyless without drugs, and so the brain sends a message to seek out something to bring the dopamine levels back up to "normal." But now there is no "normal" for the brain, because it has already begun to be affected by the drugs. Larger amounts of the substance are now needed to create that high, or dopamine flood. This is known as tolerance. Tolerance is one of the symptoms of addiction.

According to the National Institute on Drug Abuse (NIDA), "These brain changes drive a person to seek out and use drugs compulsively, despite negative consequences such as stealing, losing friends, family problems, or other physical or mental problems brought on by drug abuse—this is addiction."[3] One of the scariest things is that it isn't known how many times a certain person will use a certain substance before he or she becomes addicted. Because of many variables and risk factors, addiction can happen to one person faster than it happens to another. But once a person is addicted, the drug can basically begin to "take over" and the person will do things he or she never would have done in the past, such as steal, lie, and cheat. This is because the brain has changed and now demands that the goal is to go after what brings the "high"—the substance of choice.

But wait, if someone is now becoming addicted, why can't he or she simply replace the drug of choice with a natural high? That seems like a perfect cure for addiction! No, that won't work. Remember that drugs cause an unusually high amount of dopamine to be released, more so than the natural highs that used to make you happy and feel good—like two to ten times the regular amount of a natural high! And this high can come on right away, as soon as the drug is ingested, and it can last longer than a natural high, too. Combine this with the use-it-or-lose-it theory—remember the example about the brain and watching TV or playing an instrument? Well now your brain seeks this intense high over and over, and this becomes a regular activity for your brain. Soon the activity becomes a habit and the person becomes addicted.

There are other changes that happen to the brain when a teen takes a substance. Research shows that drinking alcohol heavily as a teen can actually shrink the frontal lobes. Do you recall what those lobes are responsible for? Making decisions? Also, drinking alcohol heavily can impact the hippocampus, a part of the brain that deals with memory and learning.

A Teen's Feelings about
How Drugs Affected Her Personality

"I have done many wrongful acts because of my destructive substance abuse. Some major things I have done due to my substance use were ending up in jail and [being] charged with my first felony for burglary and or dwelling, possession of a syringe, obstruction of an officer, lying to the law/justice system while confined, multiple disorderly conducts, battery, underage drinking. Also three probation holds and eventually renovation to serve maximum two years in a prison system and two years of extended supervision "parole" because I violated my probation rules more than I can count or comprehend. All this was a result in some way or another due to my long history of substance abuse and addition to narcotics and heroin. These wrongful sinful acts I have committed are not things I would have normally have done if it wasn't because of my drug habit. I am a kind, caring, unique individual deep down within myself when my addiction does not get in the way. I have a passion to help others and would never hurt anyone intentionally. Due to my substance abuse that person within me was turned into a manipulative and cunning baffling liar, an intelligent criminal, a person that would do anything or everything to get what I wanted and a disgusting sick individual all in results to being controlled and deceived by a substance."—Princess Peach[4]

Studies show that it might take months for the brain to start working normally again after a teen stops drinking heavily. You read that the brain is an amazing system like a computer, right? Taking substances can start making some parts of this "computer" break down and not run correctly. It can ruin the amazing functioning of the brain. That is really scary stuff if you let yourself think about it.

Just like with other diseases, the potential to end up with the disease of addiction varies between people. Many different factors can play a part, such as the environment or the genes we are born with. But that's not all. According to NIDA, addiction is a developmental disease that typically begins in childhood or adolescence.

Studies show that it might take months for the brain to start working normally again after a teen stops drinking heavily.

No single factor determines whether a person will become addicted to drugs. The overall risk for addiction is impacted by the biological makeup of the individual—it can even be influenced by gender or ethnicity, his or her developmental stage, and the surrounding social environment (e.g., conditions at home, at school, and in the neighborhood). . . . It also may result from a constellation of early biological and social vulnerability factors, including genetic susceptibility, mental illness, unstable family relationships, and exposure to physical or sexual abuse. Still, the fact remains that early use is a strong indicator of problems ahead, among them, substance abuse and addiction.[5]

> ## ? Why Do Some People Become Addicted and Some Do Not?
>
> ◉ According to Dr. Gabor Maté, "We might say that three factors need to coincide for substance addiction to occur: *a susceptible organism; a drug with addictive potential; and stress.*[6]

The method of use (how you use a drug—inject it, snort it, drink it, etc.) can also increase its addictive potential, as well as the age of the teen when he or she first uses. Anyone of any age can become addicted, but research shows that the younger the person is when he or she uses, the more likely the use will lead to substance abuse. That's probably obvious, isn't it, given the information we know about what drugs do to the brain and the fact that the teen brain isn't even done developing?

It can be hard to tell if someone you know is using. Oftentimes, the symptoms can be barely noticeable, and you can convince yourself in your mind that what you are seeing has other answers than the person being involved in substances. Even parents have a hard time determining if their child is using. But it is important for you to know what to look for, not only for people close to you, like a sibling or a friend, but for yourself, if you have been using substances.

Warning Signs of Commonly Abused Drugs

- **Marijuana:** glassy, red eyes; loud talking, inappropriate laughter followed by sleepiness; loss of interest, motivation; weight gain or loss.
- **Depressants (including Xanax, Valium, GHB):** contracted pupils; drunk-like behavior; difficulty concentrating; clumsiness; poor judgment; slurred speech; sleepiness.
- **Stimulants (including amphetamines, cocaine, crystal meth):** dilated pupils; hyperactivity; euphoria; irritability; anxiety; excessive talking followed by depression or excessive sleeping at odd times; may go long periods of time without eating or sleeping; weight loss; dry mouth and nose.
- **Inhalants (glues, aerosols, vapors):** watery eyes; impaired vision, memory, and thought; secretions from the nose or rashes around the nose and mouth; headaches and nausea; appearance of intoxication; drowsiness; poor muscle control; changes in appetite; anxiety; irritability; lots of cans/aerosols in the trash.
- **Hallucinogens (LSD, PCP):** dilated pupils; bizarre and irrational behavior including paranoia, aggression, hallucinations; mood swings; detachment

Warning Signs That a Friend or Family Member Is Abusing Drugs

The following information is from NIDA.[7]

Drug abusers often try to conceal their symptoms and downplay their problem. If you're worried that a friend or family member might be abusing drugs, look for the following warning signs (however, if some signs don't present themselves, it doesn't mean there isn't a problem).

Physical Warning Signs of Drug Abuse

- Bloodshot eyes, pupils larger or smaller than usual.
- Changes in appetite or sleep patterns. Sudden weight loss or weight gain.
- Deterioration of physical appearance, personal grooming habits.
- Unusual smells on breath, body, or clothing.
- Tremors, slurred speech, or impaired coordination.

Behavioral Signs of Drug Abuse

- Drop in attendance and performance at work or school.
- Unexplained need for money or financial problems. May borrow or steal to get it.
- Engaging in secretive or suspicious behaviors.
- Sudden change in friends, favorite hangouts, and hobbies.
- Frequently getting into trouble (fights, accidents, illegal activities).

Psychological Warning Signs of Drug Abuse

- Unexplained change in personality or attitude.
- Sudden mood swings, irritability, or angry outbursts.
- Periods of unusual hyperactivity, agitation, or giddiness.
- Lack of motivation; appears lethargic or "spaced out."
- Appears fearful, anxious, or paranoid, with no reason.

from people; absorption with self or other objects; slurred speech; confusion.

- **Heroin:** contracted pupils; no response of pupils to light; needle marks; sleeping at unusual times; sweating; vomiting; coughing, sniffling; twitching; loss of appetite.[8]

> "No one can make you feel inferior without your consent."—Eleanor Roosevelt, First Lady, active politician, and listed as one of most widely admired people of the twentieth century

What You Can Do

If you or someone you know is concerned about addiction, it is important you seek help and guidance immediately—even if you don't see all of the signs or symptoms. Time is of the essence. Find someone you know you can trust, not another teenage friend but an adult, who will help put the person in touch with

Some Thoughts about Addiction from Adults

In my interview with Tom Frank, chief of police, he said, "The problem has overwhelmed them [teens] and has put them in such a deep hole that they become very depressed and discouraged that they will not be able to change or break the addiction. It is a very negative stigma and people would rather not talk about it openly."[9]

Pastor Janis Kinens shared, "There is a stigma for sure [with addiction], and I think that it is always a 'downward spiral.' The more regularly you use the more you alienate yourself from healthy relationships. The more that happens, the more you withdraw and use. This continues until intervention or death break the cycle."[10]

Donna Bestor Krieger, a former state drug czar, wrote, "As with many adults, teens often feel they can stop or cut down anytime they want. But they enjoy using even if it causes them problems. They often don't realize the stigma attached to their use. They think anyone that uses less is boring and they fall to the lowest common denominator—friends that use as much as they do."[11]

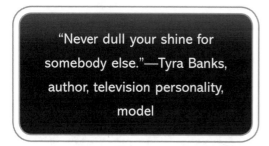

"Never dull your shine for somebody else."—Tyra Banks, author, television personality, model

a professional who deals with addiction issues. What harm can come from seeking help? I know, it might seem like you are really betraying your friend, or your brother, or even yourself, if it is you who needs the help. There might be denial and there might be fears. But what harm could come if you seek the help of an adult who can deal with this problem? What harm could come if you don't?

Admitting to a Substance Abuse Problem

Admitting to a substance abuse problem is complicated, scary, and oftentimes just plain hard to do. Often the person who has the addiction can't see it or doesn't want to face it. It has been described that facing addiction and the concept of

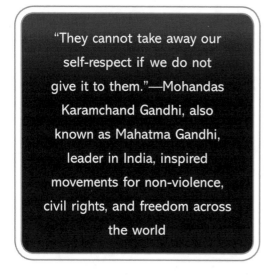

"They cannot take away our self-respect if we do not give it to them."—Mohandas Karamchand Gandhi, also known as Mahatma Gandhi, leader in India, inspired movements for non-violence, civil rights, and freedom across the world

recovery is like losing a best friend. An addict can't imagine what life would be without the substance of choice.

In an interview with Jessica, I asked if she could share her thoughts and feelings that lead up to and occurred during the time she was able to admit to having an addiction. She shared,

There were years prior where situations would happen and I'd think to myself, God, maybe I have a problem. But like we do as humans, I would feel better after a while and forget that I even went through any sort of drama or trauma. Situations would come to me or feelings of maybe this is not normal and then I would go about my life. To me, it was normal because that was my life and this is what I knew. I was comfortable with my life because I didn't know any other way of living. I thought this was how my life would go. These were just the cards I was dealt. The scenarios and my coping mechanism, of needing the substances to cope—were my cards. I was able to look in the mirror and tell myself what I thought was the truth, "You don't look so good but tomorrow you'll look better and no one can tell you are down in the dumps." When it came to realizing I had a problem, I wasn't looking for any answers. If I had my way, I would have kept doing what I thought I should be doing.

But then this voice got in touch with me, this unfamiliar yet familiar voice. It was serious and meaningful. It wasn't a suggestion that came to me. It was a necessity. It told me I needed to do this (admit I had a problem and do something about it) or I would die. At that point I felt *complete, complete* surrender. I went from being what I thought was advanced in life and knowing everything in the world, to being a beginner at life, in a split second.

So when this voice came to me, I can describe it as a white light experience. It was like something telling me, "You have a problem and you need to do something about it." The voice reoccurs. All I can describe it as is a higher power, and now I have a relationship with it. I can hear it and listen to it. The other voice I hear I now know is my disease.[12]

Treatment

When a teen has admitted to a problem, the next step is equally as crucial—what to do about it. The search for the best treatment options is ongoing.

Ryan Byrne, MD, writes about addiction treatment,

Unfortunately, there is not a huge amount of research on addiction treatment in teens. That said, the research that is available shows that the best treatment for adolescence substance abuse is treatment that involves the whole family. While many teens may not like involving parents in their treatment, we know that families are the only ones who are able to provide consistency for teen mental health treatment. It is rare teens themselves will seek out treatments. Some of the newer treatment methods are focused on a treatment called contingency management. This is a treatment plan in which a counselor or doctor will test the patient for drug or alcohol use on a weekly basis. If the teen tests positive for alcohol or drugs, she gains nothing. However, if she does prove she has not used, she earns privileges or rewards, sometimes even money. Often, treatment programs use group treatment, which means placing a group of teens with similar issues together.

Another model of treatment that I really like is called motivational enhancement therapy or motivational interviewing. This is asking questions to let the teen make their own judgments about whether substances are interfering in their lives, then lets them pick when they would like to quit, and, finally, work with them to set-up a plan of intervention.

There are no medications that have been approved for the treatment of teen substance abuse.[13]

Dealing with addictions can be a long road and one the teen must prepare him- or herself to not give up on.
Says Donna Bestor Krieger,

Recovery is tough. Many addicts go through several treatment programs which have no positive effect, at least at the time. I do not believe an addict has to hit "rock bottom" to seek recovery. In fact, if the family, friends, home is still intact, it may be easier to recover. The key is; do they want to live without their BEST FRIEND—the bottle (or drug). It is very difficult to give up that "friend" that has always been there for them. Think of it like this; you are told you may not ever see your best friend (the bottle) again. It is destructive, killing, will do you no good, ever. But in your mind, you love him. So you sneak behind the barn and meet him whenever you can. You don't really see anything wrong with him. Eventually, if you finally see the light, see what harm your friend does to you, recovery is possible.[14]

Personal Stories

Let's read about teens and their continued stories. You might notice that some of the teens admitted to having a problem, and some did not at this point.

Carol

I tried quitting a few times unsuccessfully. Then society turned against smoking. They started limiting where one could smoke. Also, what used to be fun and relaxing became something that was ruling my life. I had to be sure that I had my cigarettes along, and I had to go places that allowed smoking. I had to be sure that I didn't run out of cigarettes. Pretty soon it became more difficult to smoke than not to. Also my children were getting older and nagging me more about quitting because it bothered them. It became something that was on my mind all the time, the quitting and when and how. I guess it felt like your body and/or mind needed something—sort of like when you are really really thirsty. And too, the motions you develop when smoking, like lighting up, etc., become a big habit and if you aren't smoking you miss them. When you can finally light up, you feel a big feeling of relief and relaxation and contentment.[15]

Tim

In college I was starting to pay the consequences for my drinking. My grades were slipping. I had to leave college. I was depressed and didn't care. Everything seemed like it was hopeless. Looking back, it was more excuses than reality, but at the time, it was all real to me. I drank so much I couldn't function. I slept all day. I quit college without graduating. I went home with my tail between my legs. I was twenty-one. My parents wanted to somehow make it all better. They tried to understand it. In a way, they denied it, without even knowing they denied it.[16]

Kyle

I soon found out I was not only using drugs and alcohol but I was abusing my habit. I never thought I was addicted but I was. I would have to say the scariest situation I've been in that was related to drugs and or alcohol would have to be what I'm incarcerated for now. I was at a gas station when me and the gas station clerk began to fight. He basically insinuated that I was stealing gas from his work. Which that was not the case at all. Anyways he threatened me with calling the cops. I didn't want him to do that just for the fact I was high and a little tipsy. Seeing I am only 19 years old, I was not of legal age to consume alcohol and doing drugs is illegal, so when he stated he was calling the cops I panicked and began to take off. As I attempted to pull off, the gas station clerk decides to hang on to my car. At this point I was no longer paying any attention to him I just wanted to get out of there. So now he's got his feet inside of my car and hanging on to the open driver door. So as I am exiting the parking lot he's blocking my view of the traffic from the left. I was like "screw it I'm going to take my chance of making it across the intersection without anyone hitting me." Well that didn't work out as planned. I hit another car so now my panic level went up a couple notches. So I hit this car then continue across. I reach speeds of 50 to 55 mph then the clerk releases his grip and goes tumbling across the road. I close the door and continue driving. I'm trying to avoid all major roads so I pull over to look and see if there's any damage to the car. Nope just some scratches and no front license plate so I continued to drive back to my house in Milwaukee. A few days later the cops got me. Now I'm awaiting sentencing for 2nd degree reckless endangerment to safety and hit and run. Altogether I'm facing 13 years in prison but I took a plea for three years in prison and three years extended supervision. I'm very lucky to this very day I was not charged with murder because I could have killed the guy. I've committed crimes because of my substance abuse. I thought I was untouchable in my mind but I wasn't. I believed myself to be a good person but it was like when I was either high or drunk that overpowered me. I was told I needed help with drugs and alcohol but I didn't think I did.[17]

Princess Peach

And when we want to stop we no longer can. . . . We often do not start out abusing these drugs to the point we are killing ourselves because of our use. We simply just were experimenting. Our tolerance and expectations of using these substances change and this is the most frustrating part to us addicts. . . . The first time I ever really came to terms with myself that I had a problem with substances was probably one year in June. I had woken up with handcuff marks where they arrested me, bruises on my body and sores on my face and deep wounds where I was injecting heroin. I looked unrecognizable when I looked in the mirror, I really could not stand there and face the girl that was reflecting back at me. I had ended up catching serious criminal charges for the first time due to my use. I had lost everything that was important to me and pissed off everyone I loved and cared about and their relationships with me were broken beyond repair. I smelled, I had not remembered the last time I had bathed and cleaned myself. I reeked like stale cigarettes: I had burns from nodding out with cigarettes all over my body. Burn marks on my lips from where the crack pipe had been used. My hair was nappy and very much damaged; my teeth looked like they were not mine. I looked like I was straight up out of a horror movie, any parents' worse nightmare. I would not want to acknowledge that was my daughter either, from the horrible condition I was in. This was my first realization that I had a serious problem with substance abuse. My feelings were all the same, miserable, emotionless feelings.[18]

Jessica

But soon this "magic" of drinking and taking drugs turned into medicine for me. I needed it like a sick patient would need medicine. It became a social lubricant for me, something to help me to not think about my thoughts or feelings. Alcohol had always done that for me, but now I counted on it. If I had a drink, I didn't feel anxious and so I began to rely on it. It became my only way to socialize. My only way to fall asleep. It was my truth at the time because it was the only tool I had. By then, I was living in New York.

To most, it seemed like my dreams were coming true. I had made it to Broadway straight out of high school. It was a fast-paced city and lifestyle, and my use of marijuana kept me from being able to keep up. I was falling behind. So I changed my addiction. It was like I was dealing with five garbage cans with only four lids. When the can without the lid became stinky, I'd take off the lid of one of the covered cans and try to hide the stench of the lidless can. This only made another can stink. When marijuana began to "stink" for me, to screw up my life, I turned to something else. This was the same time that I was starting to become injured from all of my dancing. So I took percocet, a muscle relaxer, which made everything feel so much better. So instead of fixing the problem, I would mask the problem. Again, the lid of the can from one to another. When percocet was not strong enough anymore, a friend helped me start into oxycodone. To feel better, I would crush it up and snort it. That would make it work faster. But then I'd need something to level me out, because oxy made me so lethargic. To get to a normal functioning level, I started doing cocaine. I'd treat my body with one thing to lower the pain and another thing to bring my spirits higher. It was a constant balancing act. Where once I used my efforts to balance on my toes in a turn, now it seemed my efforts were to regulate what substances I'd take to keep me high yet functioning enough to move from day to day. When I was into cocaine I would make rules for myself. Like for example, I would only use if a friend offered it—my rule was that I would never buy it. But then I started hanging out with using buddies who had it all the time. So I negotiated and changed the rules. I started to buy it. I made these compromises and negotiated with myself. "Okay, you can buy cocaine but use it only at parties. At home, all you do is drink red wine." These negotiations with what at the time I thought was me bartering with me, were ongoing. I have come to learn now that I wasn't making deals with myself, but was making deals with the disease. With my addiction. But soon my rules for cocaine were gone altogether and I was using regularly. I was compulsive and would do anything to get a rush. Even steal. My dancing was excellent during this time because I couldn't even feel my body. I could just twirl and feel nothing. Pain was masked with drugs and alcohol. I felt numb. Numb not only in body but in spirit. My relationships began to suffer. Probably because I couldn't feel those either. I did a lot of hiding, both of myself and my secrets. I was insecure. I kept everyone at arm's length. My body was hurting. My relationships were hurting. I was losing everything. Each deal I made with the disease, cost me. And that's when my abuse turned into madness. There was a solid month when I was convinced that I was being watched on a reality show. Then I fully believed the government was watching me. I was paranoid. Again, I needed an escape from my thoughts that now were induced by the drugs and alcohol. By nineteen, I could make such a toxic powerful drug cocktail that I knew if I took it I could possibly die. Yet I mixed it. I took it. I didn't care.

Because of my substance abuse I was losing out on getting parts that I probably would have landed if I was not on this destructive path. One night I was at a club and I was very messed up on a variety of substances. I was out of work, unemployed. I remember being mesmerized on this red disco ball. I blacked out. When I came to, my wallet and phone were missing. The next morning I was a complete mess. A good friend took me home, made me a bloody Mary. I drank red wine, took cocaine, then weed, and went to bed. I wasted the day wasted. Again. For the last time. When I woke up that night feeling miserable, I realized that something had to change. The deal making was over. I Facebooked a friend and asked him to take me to an Alcoholics Anonymous meeting the next day. He did. It was my first AA meeting. I had nothing left. I was so desperate to get better. All I wanted was to find me. I realized that as a teen I had been struggling with identity. I was working so much that every show that I did became who I was. When I bottomed out, it was when I was not in a show. So when I was unemployed—when I didn't have a show title to identify myself as, I didn't know who I was. I was completely lost.[19]

Angela

By the time Angela was part way through high school, her mom was doing everything she could to help end what she was beginning to believe was a serious drug problem. At one point, Angela had taken a bottle of pain killers and later someone had told her if they would grind up heroin and snort it, the effect would be even better. This lead to her first experience with heroin. Angela wrote, "Finally, in late June (the summer before I became a junior), I started using heroin. I quit everything else and just used that. Heroin is my drug of choice."

Bonnie, Angela's mother, shared her memory of the time Angela was on heroin.

I thought Angela was depressed as well. I would come home from work at times and she would still be sleeping. So I had her see a psychologist/psychiatrist. I tried rewarding her for going to school. I even took off of work and shadowed her at school. Finally, I sought help from social service and local police. I found that if Angela didn't come home at curfew, I could contact the police because she was considered truant from home. They would then start searching for her. Also, if she didn't show up for school, I could call the police and have them come right into my house, into her bedroom, and escort her to school. Both of these groups were very helpful and supportive. I would punish her by taking away cell phone, Internet, and music. I would review her recent calls in and out and her text messages. I would turn her phone over to the police who would call suspicious people who had called Angela. I didn't allow her to get her driver's license. The one thing I did most was pray.

After sophomore year of Ds and Fs, Angela knew she had to make an attempt at being successful in school. When summer was ending and Angela wanted to focus back at school, she tried quitting drugs. But it wasn't that easy. Instead, she realized she was deeply addicted.

One day, Angela's mom Bonnie noticed there was $2,500 missing from her bank account. She approached Angela about it. Angela said she had stolen the money to purchase cocaine. Bonnie was no longer taking Angela's word for it, so she made Angela do a drug test. Then she told Angela that she would turn her into the police if she didn't tell her the truth. Bonnie knelt down in front of her daughter, looked her in the eyes and said, "I can't help you if you don't tell me."

Angela said, "Mom, I don't want to hurt you. If I tell you, if will be too hard for you."

But eventually, Angela said the words. "Mom, I'm addicted to heroin."

Angela's mom said, "We will get you help."

When Angela finally admitted that she was addicted to heroin, almost in the same breath Angela said, "I didn't think I'd become addicted."

The day that Angela admitted her heroin addiction to her mom is the same day she was admitted to an inpatient rehab program. Both she and her mom were intent on her becoming rehabilitated and getting her life back on track. By then, Angela's heroin addiction was consuming all she thought about and did and it was time she had intervention.

On September 17 she entered the program and spent two weeks in intense programming. Her mom visited her almost every day. The following are some of the thoughts Angela shared. The one-line answers are sentence starters Angela was asked to complete.

I am in here for heroin use and addiction. My mom found out I stole $2,500 from her checking account with her debit card. Then when she asked me what I used the money for I lied and said cocaine. She didn't believe me and threatened to send me to jail if I didn't tell her the truth so I told her about my addiction. We agreed I needed help and I was sent here. My goal for treatment would be to not have any more cravings.

I think I am pretty (sometimes).

Other people think I am a heavy drug user; a bad kid.

I feel good when I shoot up (inject heroin).

I feel bad about doing and getting addicted to heroin (and especially about taking my mom's money for it).

My parents don't understand why I use drugs.

My attitude is hopeless and negative.

Sometimes I feel guilty or ashamed about ever starting using drugs.

Sometimes I need a break from responsibilities.

Honesty is hard to be.

I have trouble stopping my heroin use.

I have frequent thoughts of wanting to inject heroin.

I worry about getting addicted again.

I get frustrated when I can't have heroin.

When I'm angry I would like other people to tell me they're sorry.

School is horrible; hell.

Using drugs/alcohol is exciting; fun; time wasters.

Write a short paragraph about thoughts or feelings you are experiencing today.

I hate feeling this way. I am restless but I can't sleep. I am craving very badly. I can't sleep. I'm bored. I'm lonely. I can't sleep.

 9/18/05

My day was average. I have been feeling cravings hardcore. I wish I could sleep. I have learned that I am very sad and emotional. I have learned that I may never stop mentally craving.

 9/19/05

My day was very emotional, a lot of crying, some anger and really happy towards the end. I love it when my mom visits. Plus I finally got to talk to my boyfriend. That was good. I've been feeling very emotional and sensitive. I've been feeling like I've had a sad life, and by reading my autobiography it makes me feel terrible about my life, it's been very sad. I've learned that I'm still a very sensitive person and the doctor said I always look like I'm about to cry when I talk to him, which is true. I have learned that I need to fill my life with other fun things instead of drugs.

 9/26/05

My day was dramatic and entertaining and happy. I've been feeling melancholy. My mom talked to my county social worker today and they are trying to get me into a school which would be nice. Sometimes to move forward on the road to recovery you have to take steps back before taking steps forward. Ps my family session with my dad was good.

10/14/05

I'd also like to talk about some problems in my life so I can de-stress. It's a long story. I guess the beginning would be during the summer when I was a heroin addict. In September I decided to go to rehab. And have been clean ever since.[20]

Arturo

By the end of the month of using prescription opiates, both of us (Angela and I) were physically addicted. I wasn't aware of this at the time because it was mild. But all I could think about was painkillers. It's all the two of us could think of or talk was painkillers. A day or so later after some phone calls we found some. We went over to the girl's house and she only wanted $20 which was cheap for prescription opiates. She pulled out two tin foil packets of brown powder. We did it, threw up, and went back to it every day that whole summer. I loved Angela but heroin was getting in between us because the two of us also loved heroin. Being addicted to heroin is like treading water. When you run out of dope you start to sink. When you finally get it you're back treading water. The whole time you're wishing you were sitting on a boat somewhere calm in the sun. The only way to get clean is to drown yourself. I went through withdrawals when Angela went to rehab in late September. I told my family I was sick. I wanted to be clean when she came back. But I was still dope sick when she got out. Angela's mom was trying to push her away from me. Rightfully so, I was a mess. That whole fall was a struggle of trying to clean up and relapse. I got an apartment and a job at an all-night diner working third shift. Things were sort of on the upswing. Angela spent a lot of time with me. We spent a lot of time listening to music.[21]

Closing This Chapter

Addiction is a heavy word. To many it used to have a stigma of failure or lack of willpower. Now, those in the know realize it is a disorder, and though the research is constantly finding new answers, it is considered a disease. Facing the truth,

"The ultimate measure of a man is not where he stands in a moment of comfort and convenience, but where he stands at times of challenge and controversy."—Dr. Martin Luther King Jr., American clergyman, activist, leader in the African American civil rights movement

though often challenging, and scary, is the first step toward living a life free of substance use.

Notes

1. Gabor Maté, *In the Realm of Hungry Ghosts: Close Encounters with Addiction* (Berkeley, CA: North Atlantic, 2010), 224.
2. Tristessa was an adult at the time of the in-person interview, 2012.
3. NIDA, "Facts on Drugs, Brain and Addiction," http://teens.drugabuse.gov/drug-facts/brain-and-addiction.
4. Princess Peach was out of high school at the time of her interview and written contribution, 2012.
5. NIDA, "Drugs, Brains, and Behavior: The Science of Addiction," http://www.drugabuse gov/publications/science-addiction/drug-abuse-addiction (accessed 2012).
6. Maté, *In the Realm of Hungry Ghosts*, 147 (italics original).
7. NIDA, "Drug Abuse and Addiction," http://www.helpguide.org/mental/drug_substance_abuse_addiction_signs_effects_treatment.htm (accessed 2012).
8. NIDA, "Drug Abuse and Addiction."
9. Tom Frank, chief of police, in response to questions I asked him, 2012.
10. Pastor Janis Kinens, Advent Lutheran Church, in response to questions I asked him, 2012.
11. Donna Bestor Krieger, former coordinator of the Alliance for a Drug-Free Wisconsin established by Governor Tommy Thompson, Attorney General Don Hanaway, and State Superintendent of Schools Herbert Grover, written contribution, 2012.
12. Jessica was an adult at the time of the interview, 2012.
13. Ryan R. Byrne, MD, assistant professor at the Medical College of Wisconsin and Child and adolescent psychiatrist at Children's Hospital of Wisconsin, in an interview and in response to questions I asked him for this book, 2012.
14. Donna Bestor Krieger, former coordinator of the Alliance for a Drug Free Wisconsin established by Governor Tommy Thompson, Attorney General Don Hanaway and State Superintendent of Schools Herbert Grover, in response to questions I asked her for this book, 2012.
15. Carol was an adult at the time of her written contribution, 2012.
16. Tim was an adult at the time of his phone interview, 2012.
17. Kyle was out of high school at the time of his written contribution, 2012.
18. Princess Peach was not in high school anymore at the time of her written contribution, 2012.
19. Jessica was a young adult at the time of her interview.
20. Angela's mom shared Angela's story and writing in an interview, 2012.
21. Arturo was a young adult at the time he shared a written interview, 2012.

RECOVERY/RELAPSE

....

"You may have to fight a battle more than once to win it."
—*Margaret Thatcher, Baroness Thatcher, prime minister
of the United Kingdom from 1979 to 1990*

Let's Talk

Addiction wouldn't be such a huge topic if recovery was simple. While the resources are great and the studies vast, there are still many perspectives on what the best recovery practices are. In this chapter, you will read about resources, insights, methods, and ideas on recovery and relapse and back on the road to recovery again.

The First Step

Admitting you have a problem is the first step toward healing, which you read about in the last chapter. For someone to admit he or she has a substance abuse disorder, he or she has to come to terms with some pretty scary truths. This can be extremely difficult. But when you know you have a problem and you've admitted it to yourself, you are now on a new path of recovery. The next step is to tell someone else.

Medical doctor Ryan Byrne says, "I believe the first step is to tell an adult that you have a problem. For the most part, this adult should be a parent or someone who could help you tell your parents that you have a substance abuse problem. As angry as parents may seem to be if they learn you are using a substance, they will forever be grateful that you decided to tell them you needed help instead of losing you to substance use."[1]

After you've admitted to having a problem, the next step is determining the course of action. Most likely it will be a course that involves treatment, either an outpatient or an inpatient program. What if you don't really want treatment?

Admitting you have a problem means you can finally get help.

Well, the verdict is still out on the effectiveness of treatment when you aren't committed to getting well. Some studies show that people who enter into a rehab program because the court ordered them to, or because their family members or other people that love them pressured them to, may eventually benefit from the treatment program despite not buying into it. However, other resources say that the person with the substance abuse issues must be committed to recovery before the programs can make an impact.

Your Brain and Recovery

Remember that the cortex is the part of the brain that involves memory and judgment, and helps us think conscious thoughts. The midbrain is the part that helps us with our drives such as hunger, thirst, sex, and pain. Unlike the cortex, conscious thoughts do not originate in the midbrain, but instead, pressure from the midbrain is sent to the cortex where that pressure is turned into conscious thought such as "Ouch, that hurts!" When the brain becomes addicted, the midbrain takes on another function, a drive for the substance. (I know, we've gone over this, but you are reading about it in a different way in case you missed it the first few times around.) The brain makes it feel like the drive for a substance is just like any one of the other drives, like the need for food, for instance. In other words, the brain tells the body it needs the substance in order to survive. Let me repeat that. *Your brain has changed so that it is now wired to demand more drugs in order to survive.* But wait, there's more. This drive becomes so powerful it overshadows the others! It can be even stronger than the hunger drive! And while the other drives are a natural way to preserve the Self, this chemically induced demand does the opposite and has the power to destroy. It has the power to kill.

So the midbrain is sending these messages to the cortex through the motor cortex. The motor cortex controls movement. This drives action. The impaired frontal lobe won't stop the person from the action. The messaging goes to the cortex as a craving for drugs, and the addicted person heeds that craving and then takes an action, and it translates as the addicted person getting in a car, for example, and driving to the dealer to buy some drugs.

It is important to point out that there is a part of this whole process when the brain tries to interpret the action or analyze it. But it is usually no match for the strong drive for drugs, and the cycle continues.

So what does it take for treatment to be effective? How can treatment overpower the strong drives of an addiction? In simple terms, some believe it means bringing the midbrain and the cortex into alignment with each other, so that they agree on a common goal. The midbrain is dealing with survival and convincing the cortex into believing that feeding the addiction is what will keep that body going. So the midbrain has to come on board and cooperate. But first, most experts agree, the addict must stop the behavior.

Withdrawal can occur when substance use is suddenly stopped and is an important part of the treatment. Often it is very important to have professionals involved in the withdrawal process. Without using the substances, the brain will return to a more normal state, which will help the person feel calm and have a sense of well-being. This takes time. It can take months and sometimes even years. And there is, of course, more to this all than this handful of sentences can explain. After time and healing take place, ideally the person then works through the thoughts, the rationalization, the excuses that helped feed the addiction. Finally the person is able to see clearly what the addiction did and has the power to do, which was to control, to destroy. It is at this point that the addict begins to see how the substance affected his or her brain's natural chemistry and finally, balance takes over and the addictive drive subsides. The person can then deal with his or her feelings and emotions and hopefully starts to see life, the Self—everything—from a different perspective. There are other parts of the brain, other factors, and new discoveries that are happening that play a part in rehab. But understanding even a layer of it helps.

Wait, did I mention the word *neuroplasticity* yet? When you read about the use-it-or-lose-it idea? When you read about habit and patterns? It's a super cool word

How can treatment overpower the strong drives of an addiction?

and one you might want to consider keeping in your brain. Well, neuroplasticity is the amazing power of your brain to be able to form new neural connections to basically reorganize them. In this way, the brain is able to compensate for injury and disease.

Here's another great term, one you might like even better than neuroplasticity: *neural pathway*. Neural pathways are like roads in your brain. The more you travel these roads, the more familiar your brain becomes with these roads and the more solid these pathways become. Recall the warm chocolate chip cookie? If you woke up every morning and went straight to that cookie jar, grabbed a cookie, munched it down, and then went about your morning, that whole cookie scenario would form a pathway in your brain so that when you awakened, this is what your

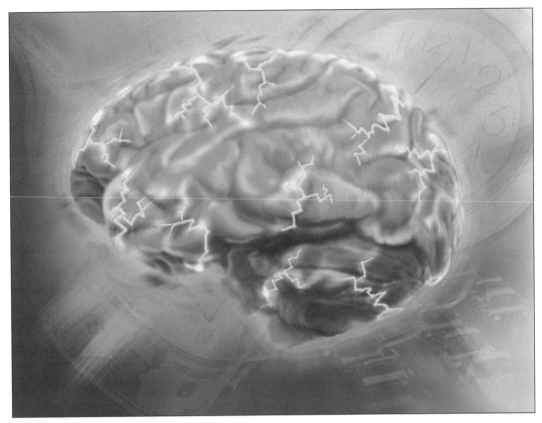

Your brain can build new pathways.

body would want you to do. Get up and grab that cookie. You now have this as a neural pathway.

But wait, are the roads in your life already all paved? Is life now an unending set of patterns of various cookie-grabbing events?

Ever hear of that old saying, "Take the road less traveled"? Well, the great, amazing news is our brains can build new pathways—the road(s) less traveled! That means that we can create new habits and that means, yes, we can get rid of the old . . . like addictions. What's this all called again? Neuroplasticity of the brain. Good thinking.

So, we can rewire our brain; reprogram it in a way, if you will. We can forge new paths we haven't been on before. So why not give this a little trial? It's so simple to do. Just try something you haven't done before (ahem . . . non-substance related, of course) such as throwing that backpack over your left shoulder instead of your right shoulder. It might seem weird, off balance, odd. That's because you have a neural pathway that tells your Self to toss that backpack onto your right shoulder. It's what some think of as a brainless act. You don't even consciously think of it. Trying something a new way, like hoisting that pack on to your left shoulder, is opening up the possibility of building a new pathway. Plus, it will affect your physical body differently (those muscles that haven't been used on the left side now will be getting a little attention). So even this simple act of backpack transition is creating a new neural pathway. Now, imagine how this all could affect the addicted brain!

In the amount of time it has taken to write the words that you just read, scientists somewhere on this planet are coming up with new discoveries about the human brain, about the body, about the brains in the body and how they all work together.

It's All Coming Together

The bottom line is this: you can read any statistic that you want to about substance addiction, the failure rate, the deaths and the unending cycles of the disorder. But keep in mind that our minds are unlimited, and we haven't yet discovered everything yet to be discovered. Though we have a lot of facts and figures that lead people to believe certain things about the disorder, one thing that can never be a statistic is the ability of the human. The brain is an amazing part of the human body, but I mean the brain working in conjunction with the body and that other essence (that people call different things such as spirit, life force, soul) that makes someone who he or she is. These three components—body, brain, and essence—

YOU are unlimited potential.

can help define us as "human," and when they work together, our potential is unlimited. It's true—there's one thing we can't prove as a fact or a figure and that is the potential of this unified package. That's right. And that's *you*. YOU are unlimited potential.

Some people start to get a little itchy and squirrely when you mix science and what people deem as nonscience (something that can't be proven, like what a "soul" is made up of) together into one recipe, but sometimes there comes a time (like right now in this book) when it all comes together and comes out tasting and

Consider This . . .

"In the early part of the twentieth century, there was a paradigm regarding the four-minute mile. It was said, and almost everyone believed, that it was impossible for a human to run a mile in under four minutes. Doctors of that era said that the human physiology would break down and kill a runner before that could be accomplished. Engineers said that the aerodynamics of the human body made it impossible for someone to run a mile in under four minutes."[2]

Throughout history, thousands of people tried to break this running record. No one succeeded. Indeed, it seemed impossible for a human to run a mile in under four minutes. Why? Was it truly because the human body was made in such a way that it was impossible? Or was it something else? Could it have been because of the power of a paradigm?

Roger Bannister, on May 6, 1954, completed a mile run in three minutes, 59.4 seconds. John Landy completed the mile in three minutes, 58 seconds, a mere six weeks after Bannister. John Walker has run the mile in less than four minutes more than one hundred times.

What happened? Why was what once was thought of impossible now becoming a common occurrence? "It's not that the runners were faster or stronger; it's that they believed it could be done. That's what happens to a paradigm, and to any belief system, when a hole is blown in it. Everyone pours through the gap in the new way of thinking."[3]

looking like something we've never tried before. Like I said, the brain, body, and human essence make up a powerful package.

Do you know what a paradigm is? It's kind of like an assumption. Kind of like a way of thinking in a certain pattern. Think back to when you read about building new neural pathways?

Are there certain paradigms around addiction? Can we run the mile in less than four minutes? If you are in the midst of an addiction or suffering with a lack of hope because of a strong belief in the inability of someone to get better with an addiction, let's hear it for building new neural pathways, for the smashing of paradigms, and, my friends, for honoring the amazing human potential that *you* are!

You Want to Recover, But Is It Possible?

What if you really want to recover? You want nothing more than to be free of this disorder that is impacting your life in such a negative way! Not only get better, but rid yourself of the addiction. The first question that might cross your mind could be, Is there a cure for addiction? At the time that this book was written, most research said there is no "cure" and that addiction is an ongoing condition that can be controlled to live a "normal" life. That is, there is a path of recovery that can enable the individual to live a substance-free life.

What does it mean to have a chronic condition? That means that it is ongoing, so although you might not have any symptoms presenting themselves, you have the possibility of relapsing. Similar to a disease such as asthma, where a person might go into relapse and exhibit symptoms, people who are addicted could do so as well. So it is an ongoing process of working on wellness and well-being. If you or someone you know has not yet had success recovering, that doesn't mean you won't ever have success!

Myths or Facts?

Many people believe that addiction is all about the lack of willpower. If you really want to stop using, you can. But research states that this isn't fact. As you have learned in the previous chapters, addiction changes the brain, and the reality is that prolonged exposure to drugs creates powerful cravings and a desire to use. This alteration of brain function affects the success of quitting by the use of willpower.

Another belief that people have is that addiction is a disease, and therefore, you might as well resign yourself to a life of continued use because there is nothing that can be done about it. While many experts agree that addiction is a disease, there are brain changes that do occur with addiction that can be treated and even reversed through various therapies, treatments, and practices.

So When Is the Best Time to Begin Treatment?

You've probably heard the phrase, "No time like the present." You've probably also heard, "You have to hit rock bottom before you can begin to recover." So when *is* the best time to begin seeking treatment? Do you have to have nowhere to go but up before you will have any success in healing? Actually, it turns out that the "no time like the present" concept wins hands down. The earlier, the better when it comes to a substance abuse treatment plan, but certainly, recovery can begin at any point in the process. The longer someone abuses substances, the stronger the problem can become and the more challenging it can be to recover. Whenever you begin to seek help, it isn't too soon. And hopefully, it isn't too late. But take action *now*.

Treatment

Some say that their "addiction" became their best friend, and the idea of turning from that one thing that gives them pleasure, self-confidence, and a feeling of comfort is dreadfully scary. This is where treatments come in. You'll have knowledgeable people who can help you see things from a different perspective and help you address the issues that are preventing you from living a full life because of the substances. You'll also be able to get to know people who are going through or who have been through what you are going through. All of this will help you, comfort you, and allow you to begin to rely on yourself, instead of the substance, to sustain you. Many consider this to be the greatest freedom. Even if you aren't feeling confident about this right now, taking the first step to seek treatment will help. People are trained to assist those with substance abuse disorder to see what the substance has been doing to them, their relationships, and their lives, and can help them see that their addiction isn't such a best friend after all.

Treatment for addictions comes in all sorts of shapes and sizes. There are a variety of approaches, plans, philosophies, and facilities (both inpatient, where you would stay at the facility while you get treatment, and outpatient, where you would go somewhere for treatments but not stay overnight). You will read about them later on in the book to help you see that the choices are many, and you are encouraged to do research beyond this book, as well.

Principles of Drug Addiction Treatment: A Research-Based Guide (Third Edition)[4]

Research on what makes addiction treatments successful is ongoing. Here are some principles of drug addiction treatment from NIDA:

1. Addiction is a complex but treatable disease that affects brain function and behavior. Drugs of abuse alter the brain's structure and function, resulting in changes that persist long after drug use has ceased. This may explain why drug abusers are at risk for relapse even after long periods of abstinence and despite the potentially devastating consequences.

2. No single treatment is appropriate for everyone. Treatment varies depending on the type of drug and the characteristics of the patients. Matching treatment settings, interventions, and services to an individual's particular problems and needs is critical to his or her ultimate success in returning to productive functioning in the family, workplace, and society.

3. Treatment needs to be readily available. Because drug-addicted individuals may be uncertain about entering treatment, taking advantage of available services the moment people are ready for treatment is critical. Potential patients can be lost if treatment is not immediately available or readily accessible. As with other chronic diseases, the earlier treatment is offered in the disease process, the greater the likelihood of positive outcomes.

4. Effective treatment attends to multiple needs of the individual, not just his or her drug abuse. To be effective, treatment must address the individual's drug abuse and any associated medical, psychological, social, vocational, and legal problems. It is also important that treatment be appropriate to the individual's age, gender, ethnicity, and culture.

5. Remaining in treatment for an adequate period of time is critical. The appropriate duration for an individual depends on the type and degree of the patient's problems and needs. Research indicates that most addicted individuals need at least 3 months in treatment to significantly reduce or stop their drug use and that the best outcomes occur with longer durations of treatment. Recovery from drug addiction is a long-term process and frequently requires multiple episodes of treatment. As with other chronic illnesses, relapses to drug abuse can occur and should signal a need for treatment to be reinstated or adjusted. Because individuals often leave treatment prematurely, programs should include strategies to engage and keep patients in treatment.

6. Behavioral therapies—including individual, family, or group counseling—are the most commonly used forms of drug abuse treatment. Behavioral therapies vary in their focus and may involve addressing a patient's motivation to change, providing incentives for abstinence, building skills to resist drug use, replacing drug-using activities with constructive and rewarding activities, improving problem-solving skills, and facilitating better interpersonal relationships. Also, participation in group therapy and other peer support programs during and following treatment can help maintain abstinence.

7. Medications are an important element of treatment for many patients, especially when combined with counseling and other behavioral therapies. For example, methadone, buprenorphine, and naltrexone (including a new long-acting formulation) are effective in helping individuals addicted to heroin or other opioids stabilize their lives and reduce their illicit drug use. Acamprosate, disulfiram, and naltrexone are medications approved for treating alcohol dependence. For persons addicted to nicotine, a nicotine replacement product (available as patches, gum, lozenges, or nasal spray) or an oral medication (such as bupropion or varenicline) can be an effective component of treatment when part of a comprehensive behavioral treatment program.

8. An individual's treatment and services plan must be assessed continually and modified as necessary to ensure that it meets his or her changing needs. A patient may require varying combinations of services and treatment components during the course of treatment and recovery. In addition to counseling or psychotherapy, a patient may require medication, medical services, family therapy, parenting instruction, vocational rehabilitation, and/or social and legal services. For many patients, a continuing care approach provides the best results, with the treatment intensity varying according to a person's changing needs.

9. Many drug-addicted individuals also have other mental disorders. Because drug abuse and addiction—both of which are mental disorders—often co-occur with other mental illnesses, patients presenting with one condition should be assessed for the other(s). And when these problems co-occur, treatment should address both (or all), including the use of medications as appropriate.

10. Medically assisted detoxification is only the first stage of addiction treatment and by itself does little to change long-term drug abuse. Although medically assisted detoxification can safely manage the acute physical symptoms of withdrawal and can, for some, pave the way for effective long-term addiction treatment, detoxification alone is rarely sufficient to

help addicted individuals achieve long-term abstinence. Thus, patients should be encouraged to continue drug treatment following detoxification. Motivational enhancement and incentive strategies, begun at initial patient intake, can improve treatment engagement.

11. Treatment does not need to be voluntary to be effective. Sanctions or enticements from family, employment settings, and/or the criminal justice system can significantly increase treatment entry, retention rates, and the ultimate success of drug treatment interventions.

12. Drug use during treatment must be monitored continuously, as lapses during treatment do occur. Knowing their drug use is being monitored can be a powerful incentive for patients and can help them withstand urges to use drugs. Monitoring also provides an early indication of a return to drug use, signaling a possible need to adjust an individual's treatment plan to better meet his or her needs.

13. Treatment programs should test patients for the presence of HIV/AIDS, hepatitis B and C, tuberculosis, and other infectious diseases as well as provide targeted risk-reduction counseling, linking patients to treatment if necessary. Typically, drug abuse treatment addresses some of the drug-related behaviors that put people at risk of infectious diseases. Targeted counseling focused on reducing infectious disease risk can help patients further reduce or avoid substance-related and other high-risk behaviors. Counseling can also help those who are already infected to manage their illness. Moreover, engaging in substance abuse treatment can facilitate adherence to other medical treatments. Substance abuse treatment facilities should provide onsite, rapid HIV testing rather than referrals to offsite testing—research shows that doing so increases the likelihood that patients will be tested and receive their test results. Treatment providers should also inform patients that highly active antiretroviral therapy (HAART) has proven effective in combating HIV, including among drug-abusing populations, and help link them to HIV treatment if they test positive.

Behavioral Treatments[5]

Obviously, if using substances is what is causing the distress in your life, then stopping them is the goal. Behavioral treatments involve teaching the patient new lifestyle habits, developing new patterns, and letting go of the old. One approach, called cognitive-behavioral therapy deals with people's thoughts, feelings, and emotions. It involves teaching patients to deal with their own Self—how they feel, react, and think about things—versus reacting to outside forces, like other people, events that happen, and environments that all might trigger a response. Educating the individual on how to deal with feelings and thoughts, and how to turn that into action versus reaction, can be a part of the therapy as well. Some of these incorporate relaxation techniques.

Family Therapy[6]

Family therapy means getting family members involved by learning how to best respond to the person going through treatment. Having a support group surrounding the patient can help in getting well.

Pharmaceutical Treatments[7]

This approach deals with using medications to ease an individual off of drugs or maintain a place of balance. The goal is to help the individual live a productive life without the focus being substances use.

Faith-Based Recovery

Faith-based recovery is another available approach. This is one in which the treatment plan is based on a specific religion. It can be beneficial for many because instead of feeling like an outsider at meetings and gatherings, people are able to relate to others with this common belief that they all share. For the first time for many, they are in a setting in which they feel accepted. In addition, the idea of turning to a faith that encourages a belief that there is a power greater than oneself, and therefore greater than the addiction, can be healing.

Yvonne Dennis, a social worker and author of more than ten books and someone who has worked with those suffering from addiction disorders, shared her thoughts on this healing modality in an interview. She believes that faith-based recovery will help some of those afflicted find success in healing. "We all know of the physical part of an addiction, but it is also a spiritual disease. Some people have always felt like outsiders, so when they are able to be among others that practice their same tradition or have the same belief system, they finally fit in, which can be a key factor in being able to withstand the struggles of recovery." Dennis said that she likes to expose individuals to various methods of healing, from holistic, to faith based. She compares it to shopping in a department store. She doesn't care what department someone shops in, as long as he or she comes out with something they've been "sold." She thinks it is important a person has something to believe in that is greater than the addiction, which can include believing in one's own inner worth. Someone suffering needs something to hang on to, something that resonates with him or her. Dennis goes on to share that while she believes it is important to have something greater than the addiction to believe in, a sense of interconnectedness is also important. This goes back to the idea of feeling a part of something. She shares, "Being a part of something isn't just receiving; it is giving back. It is realizing that the exchange itself is an important part of the process."

Dennis goes on to say, "Personally, I believe in the connectedness and harmony of the universe—we are all related to each other, to the plants, mountains, waters, other animals, etc. To me, if we understand that connection and 'relatedness,' it can be a key to healing, to developing a sense of interconnectedness. Our goal on this earth, to me, is not to be independent, or dependent, our goal is to be interdependent with all of creation. A symbiotic relationship with the world."

How does this come into play when it relates to seeking a recovery program? Dennis believes the first step is allowing others (those qualified) to help.

> There are many instances when we have trust in others. When we get onto a bus, we believe the bus driver will take us to the place we need to go. We believe he or she will not get lost, will drive safely, and will abide by all of the laws of a bus driver. We do trust. We have it in our soul to be interdependent. It is part of who we are. That's what we need to remember when it comes to treatment. We need to understand that we can trust others to help us, and when the time is right, and we've accepted help from others, we will offer others our help in return. People who believe in harm reduction know that there is interconnectedness in life. They realize that everyone has a responsibility to themselves, the earth, and to each other. We are all connected. There is a certain amount of accountability in living this life.

The approach Dennis speaks of incorporates the idea that it takes the community to help with what some feel is an epidemic. As Dennis shares, addiction is indeed the opposite of working together. Addiction is a selfish disease.

> Can you see how addiction is a selfish disease? Someone, who is being driven by an addiction, is rarely able to put someone else in front of the addiction. Actually, often puts his or her own well-being second to addiction. It is the addiction that is fed, nurtured, and hung onto at the cost of so much. This isn't to say that it is the person's nature to be selfish. This is to say that the addiction itself is selfish. And right now, the society we live in is by and large, selfish. The goal is to get the biggest house, the most money, the highest degree. Addiction treatments we talked about go against this—instead it fosters the idea that it takes the community, the

Faith-Based Recovery

Some choose a faith-based recovery program as a stand-alone program. Others find it or bring it into another recovery treatment. Faith, religion, and spirituality can be integrated into these methods and the holistic ones you'll learn about in the next chapter.

The scope of world religions is great. Often the messages within a faith can resonate and help guide recovery. The following messages are from various religious or spiritual leaders and might be inspiring for someone struggling to find his or her way out of addiction.[8]

"Truth is high, higher still is truthful living!"—Guru Nanak, founder of Sikhism, Sikhism

"For thirty years I sought God. But when I looked carefully I found that in reality God was the seeker and I the sought."—Bistami, philosopher and mystic, Islam, Sufism

"To cease to be identified with the body, to separate oneself from the body-consciousness, is a recognized and necessary step whether toward spiritual liberation or toward spiritual perfection and mastery over Nature."—Aurobindo Ghose, philosopher, poet, and mystic, Hinduism

"Return to the origin and keep to the origin."—Ho Shang Gong, Daoism

"Wishing to establish his own character, he also establishes the character of others, and wishing to be prominent himself, he also helps other to be prominent."—Confucius, founder of Confucianism

"For truly, I say to you, if you have faith as a grain of mustard seed, you will move this mountain, 'Move from here to there,' and it will move; and nothing will be impossible to you."—Jesus Christ, founder of Christianity

"Everything good and bad comes from your own mind. To find something beyond the mind is impossible."—Bodhidharma, founder of Chan Buddhism, Buddhism, Mahayana, Zen (Chan)

family, a culture, to be aware and support the addict towards recovery. Again . . . it's all about feeling a part of the whole. It goes back to the interconnectedness.[9]

Resources for Resources[10]

Besides the many resources that offer treatments, ideas, support, and information, there are even services that help you or the addicted person find services. For example, the Substance Abuse and Mental Health Services Administration sponsors the Behavioral Health Treatment Services Locator. A service like this can help you determine what treatment would best serve your needs. A program that suits you might mean a two-week program to begin with or it might mean something more along the lines of a holistic approach. Finding something that is right for you is an important part of healing.

Substance addiction can be treated by therapies that are behavioral based. Programs that match the individual's needs can be successful but not always successful on the first try. Many need repeat programs to achieve success. Recovery isn't a one-step process for many people. Some try, are on the path of recovery, and then relapse. That doesn't mean it is a sign to throw in the towel and give up. Use the relapse as a cue to get back in there, either using the same approach or trying something else.

More Treatment Options

At the back of this book you'll find resources that can help you on your search for treatment programs. Additionally, in the next chapter you will find other types of therapies and methods that you may opt to seek out and engage in to further your path toward healing.

Experiences of Teens

Recovery and *relapse* are words very familiar to those people with substance abuse disorders. They are also common terms for family members, friends, and coworkers involved with someone struggling with substances. Read what teens have to say about recovery and relapse. Some of these interviews were given by teens and some by adults who remember their teen experiences and share with us how those experiences have affected their adult years.

Carol

Finally I decided to just get the quitting over with. I went to a hypnotist who hypnotized me and gave me a tape to play several times a day. Well, I lost the tape somewhere so that didn't work. I bought various items that were supposed to help you quit, cigarette holders that you dialed down the nicotine, a little machine that told you when you could smoke etc., etc. None of those things worked. Somehow I got ahold of the name of a lady who worked with people on a 12-step kind of program. I went to see her even though she was about an hour's drive away. The program had a workbook and let you smoke for about 2 or 3 weeks while cutting back on the amounts. The program let you know that the cigarette, what we all thought of as our friend who did all these things with us, really was not a friend because of the hurt it could do. After 3 weeks we said goodbye to the cigarettes and flushed them down the toilet. I went to see this lady and worked the workbook for several months. Between her, the program, and many, many prayers asking God to take away the yearning to smoke, I quit for good. Actually, I told myself that I was only choosing to not smoke for that hour, then that day, etc., and that when I was 72 years old I could smoke again. Well, I am 72 now and choose not to. Because I had asthma as a child and I smoked, I developed COPD [chronic obstructive pulmonary disease] and am now on O_2 [oxygen] 24 hours a day. Because of my illness I am sorry that I ever took that first cigarette but to be honest, I did enjoy smoking. But let me tell you, enjoyment or not, it was not worth it. Not being able to breathe is the worst thing that can happen to someone. It really changes your life. If I had my life to live over, I would not ever smoke that first cigarette.[11]

Tim

I took a semester off of school, I stopped drinking, went back to school. I thought I was fine, that I was back to normal. So I believed I could go back to drinking casually. But I ended up in the same spot that I was in. I realized I wasn't solving an issue, I was just putting it aside. You think you have this little problem, and if you deal with it a certain way, it will just go away, but it doesn't. When I was bored I would drink. I'd drink a couple of beers, no big deal, but when you are in a destructive mode, you can always find that person who will do it with you and won't encourage you to stop. I'd find that person. I would never choose someone strong enough to tell me I was screwing up.

Friends along the way said drinking is destructive and I realize that relationships don't last for a reason. Eventually, the person you choose to be with is either drunk with you or is leaving you.

I took forever to graduate because of the same process. I lost a lot of years of my life.

By the time I was nearing my midtwenties, I figured out I had a problem. It was a repeat, the same thing over and over. For most people, messing up once is acceptable and they don't do it again, but I continued to do the same stupid thing over and over (like missing class because of drinking) then you realize there is something wrong with you.

Eventually I stopped again, but I would then start again. You have no control. You know it is wrong and you don't want to but you also don't care. I was a smoozer so I could do no wrong, so I could get away with things like missing work. I was being enabled.

You become a black hole. You wake up and you realize, what just happened to those five years? You look and the mirror and say, "Where have I been?"

I was a binger for years and years. I would stop but then when I would go back to drinking, I would drink a lot. I would start because of boredom or you think you got it licked, your body thinks it's smarter than you are. "Now I'm past this, now I can do what I want." To yourself, you don't see it as grave as it really is. You don't address, you don't admit it fully. You know it but you won't admit it to outside people so you keep pretending. And they keep enabling.

Fast-forward to the present. I am laying in a hospital bed saying, "What in the hell am I doing here?" I'm preparing for a liver transplant. I have to be sober for six months. It is usually a year-and-a-half process. I know I can't drink anymore or I will die. I am forty-seven years old.[12]

Princess Peach

I have been in many scary situations due to my drug use; probably the most scariest situation I can recognize would be over the course of this year. It was April 11, 2012. I had just left work, went home sick because I was physically sick from using my drug of choice, heroin. I was going through bad withdrawals from not using heroin in the past two days, I was trying to quit yet again such as many failed attempts prior to this. I went home to my apartment and I had a guy meet me at my home to help medicate me to hopefully help stop the withdrawals. He had picked up two bags of heroin. That really is not a lot from what my tolerance was back then. I just previously had been released from jail. I was only a week out. So I have heard plenty of horror stories and also have had a few friends overdose because they couldn't handle the same amount that they use to be able to use and ended up dying or close to it. I never planned that day being another statistic. I had said the guy came by to medicate and gave me the heroin to use. I cooked it up in the small silver tin and stirred it around with the plunger of the syringe and I remember making a comment to him that is looked like a strong batch. He said it was like the batch we got three days earlier and when I used that time I was completely incoherent that night so I knew maybe it was not such a good idea to use the whole amount in the bag. I should just do half and the horror stories were running in the back of my heart at this moment. Well here's the thing; addiction doesn't care about horror stories or whether or not it is a strong batch and you should use less this time. I stirred the brown liquid up, put the litter underneath the sliver tin cooker, and sucked up the mixture in the syringe. I had a passion of playing doctor when it came to my obsession heroin. I would joke about that all the time, that one day I would make a good nurse. "Syringes," they're typically used by heroin user ha! I really wish I never said that because within moments I had, as I was saying, finished mixing the heroin, I sucked up the liquid as said, and I tied a blue tourniquet, "the kind at the doctor," to my wrist. I had injected the heroin in the wound from my last use in my hand. I insistently hit the vein and watched the blood fall from my hand and I put the cap back on the syringe and tried licking the blood off so it would not get on the floor. Within minutes, I had the famous "rush" that all heroin junkies get and I began to "nod out, fade in and out of consciousness." The guy had stepped outside, that's all I remember last, and I had a cigarette in one hand unlit prior to losing consciousness. Within five minutes of using the heroin, I blacked out and was unresponsive. The guy had come back and I was completely white as a ghost and my lips he said were lipstick blue. He thought I was messing around at first, so he started to hit me but I was not responding. He then said I was making gasping noises because I was losing oxygen and could not breathe. He then called 911 nervously because I hated all authority figures and the law but also because he had really thought he had killed me and was scared he'd be sitting behind bars and never getting out! That he ended a young girl's life due to a heroin overdose.

The paramedics came with law enforcement, it stated in the police report, and they tried to revive me. They were about to put a breathing tube in me but I had denied it and I arose from my death. I woke up from my near fatal overdose with police and a paramedic woman standing over me on my floor in my apartment. I was in great shock that I nearly killed myself and was quite frightened what the consequemces were going to result in this. They put me on a stretcher and rushed me to the emergency room, where I was administered Narcain, "a drug used to contradict the heroin" and stop the drug from killing me in my body. I was given that because I was still dying when I was entering the hospital. After I was re-vived for the second time that day, I was all shaken up by almost dying that evening. The guy picked me up and I went back to my apartment against what the doctors had recommended and discharged without consent. I poured myself grape soda and vodka to calm my nerves and watched the evening news with him like nothing had ever happened. He had said that my overdose had scared him greatly and he was glad I was alive. I looked at him and said I wanted to use heroin again and couldn't deal with what just took place earlier that evening. My addiction and obsession to heroin almost ended my life and I still wanted to get high? That is the most sick-ening thing I have ever said and this was the scariest situation I have been in in using substances.[13]

Jessica

I am just now getting to know me and my feelings. When I was fourteen is the last time I was in touch with who I was. Being on substances [since] then stopped my emotional development, so I have to go back and learn how to deal with fourteen-year-old feelings. At one time I was self-seeking and dishonest. But I realize now, that that didn't make me up, that those actions and attributes were by products of an untreated disease. It wasn't me. One of the scariest and, I think, truest things about alcoholism is that is sounds like you. The ideas to use sound like your ideas. It sounds like you negotiating with yourself. But it is not. It is you negotiating with the disease. For me, I realize, there is no cure. But there certainly is way to get better. Programs like AA [Alcoholics Anonymous]. Not a pill you take to get well. Now I know it is the life you live to get well.

Now, for the first time in my life I am able to access my emotions, instead of manufacturing them as an actor. It makes me present on stage. And I know I will get well one day at a time. All I have is today and this moment. I am now able to feel my body and feel what is going on in my body instead of going numb. Now I practice being present and I can assess what my body is doing and not judge it. I can think about how to fix it now. I'm learning how to take care of myself. At the time this book was being written, I had been sober for six months. I am still an artist. I dance, I act, I sing. But now my art is something else for me instead of an escape. It is a part of me, a way to express my truth. It helps me to be more present. It has helped me to observe my thoughts and let them go without judgment. My dreams that I had as a young girl to be a famous dancer or actor are no longer. I know what that is like. Now, my dream is to be me, in every thought that I have, in every action I take. In every moment that I live. I know I can and will continue to be successful at that. Most importantly, being true to myself, I can be true to others. When I love myself, I can love others.[14]

Angela

Angela spent two weeks in substance abuse rehab. Part of her therapy was to write about her addiction:

My needs being met when I use are to have fun, and add excitement to my life. I use when I am feeling every emotion; ex: if I am happy I'll use to make me extremely happy, or I'll use when I am stressed to take my mind off of things for a bit or I'll use when I'm feeling really energized to help me sleep or when I'm feeling unmotivated to help me feel motivated . . . and these are just some examples.

The effects of drug use on my behavior: unmotivated, irritable towards anyone who gets in my way of using, and my brain becomes concerned with one thing—Heroin. Instead of concentrating on myself I just concentrate on Heroin. My relationships with people who use when I am using become almost non-existent, my relationship with my mom deteriorates, and my relationship with my boyfriend becomes a mess of fights about unimportant and useless fights about money and drugs. All I think about in school is using, and heroin takes a large toll on my physical, emotional and mental health.

Mom, there's not a way amazing enough to start this letter to show how special you are. You are the most caring, supportive, giving, responsible organized person, it's almost unhuman. Anyways, now that I've schmoozed you I'd like to apologize for stealing your money for something as useless and unmeaningful as drugs, and also to tell you not to blame yourself, for any of my actions. Whatever happens to separate us in our lives, whether it be miles or emotions, or life or death, I'll always love you. You'll never leave my thoughts. I appreciate everything you do. Love, Angela.

Five to ten things I can do to reduce cravings draw, write, listen to music, go shopping, and spend all my money so I can't buy it, or exercise.

I have a good way of transferring my cravings onto paper, whether it's art or writing. I am committed to taking my addiction one day at a time and starting each new day fresh.

After the two-week program was complete, Angela went to an alternative school that allowed her to continue working toward her high school diploma while not being immersed in the same environment with the same peers that she was involved with when she had been using. Angela did remarkably well. She never missed a day of school. She became an impeccable dresser again. On September 13 she had turned seventeen, and so on November 29, her mom, proud of her progress and success, suggested this be the day that Angela get her driver's license.

On November 29, Angela came down from her bedroom dressed in a long camel pleated skirt. She had a gold colored vest with a white blouse underneath, and camel and brown pumps with great big gold buttons. Her dreadlocks were pulled back with an ivory ribbon in her hair. Her mom dropped her off at school, watching her daughter walk the long path to enter the building.

It was planned that Angela's stepdad would pick her up and take her to get her driver's license, but Angela called her mom during the day and said that a custodian had to bring her, so Bonnie made arrangements to leave work early. They met at home, and once again, Angela walked down the stairs, this time dressed in jeans and a pink sweater. When her mom asked her why she had changed, she said, "Oh, I have to look like a teenager."

Angela passed her test that day. She was ecstatic. She and her mom drove home chatting about the day. Her mom said to her, "Wow, this is an Angela day." All was good. Angela had stopped using. She had graduated from her rehab program. She was doing well in school again, was responsible, was dressing and sleeping like she used to, and now had her driver's license. Her mom gave her twenty dollars and suggested she and her boyfriend get some dinner and she would see them later at home.

Angela's curfew was 8:30 p.m., and when she didn't come home then, Bonnie called and a friend said they'd be back shortly. They were. When Angela walked through the door, she was acting fine. But she wasn't looking fine. She looked like her eyes were greener, like her irises were larger. Her mom became suspicious. Angela reassured her she had taken her sleeping medication. She checked the mileage on the car and wondered how Angela had put on over eighty miles. When she confronted Angela, Angela became defensive. Her mom told Angela that she couldn't use the car in the morning. Bonnie left Angela to go to sleep.

But that night, something still bothered her mom. So Bonnie went into her daughter's room. Hearing the labored breathing from what she thought was a cold, she quietly went through Angela's backpack, relieved that she didn't find anything.

The next morning, Bonnie called to hurry Angela along to get ready for school. Angela didn't reply, so her mom went into her bedroom. She rested her hand on her daughter's shoulder to waken her up. And that's when she saw Angela's purple lips.

Sometime between one in the morning and six, Angela had died. Only three months after the first time she used heroin. She left behind a mother, a father, and a younger brother.

Later her friends said she had used the twenty dollars for what she claimed was "her last use of heroin, to celebrate getting her license."

Angela's mom says, "I remember looking at some of Angela's homework after she had died. She had finished her treatment in September and I was flipping over homework from the middle of November. I felt so overwhelmed with pain when I saw a small phrase on the backside of one of her assignments. She had written, 'I miss heroin.' I can only imagine the battles she went through to try and stay clean. And it was a battle she had to fight alone, every single day.

Anyone who knew Angela knew how interesting she was—almost like an old soul in a young body. She was very sensitive about people or animals being mistreated. She was a bright light."[15]

Arturo

The day before Thanksgiving I relapsed again. I only remember where I was. I woke up in the hospital. I got picked up about eight hours later when the hospital finally let me go. I was still high the next day. The overdose terrified me but apparently not enough to shake the monkey off my back. A week later Angela overdosed.

She got her license that day. We were with another girl and looking for something to do. I hadn't used since the day I overdosed. One of them wanted to go down. I didn't argue. I was hopeless. The girls we were with called a friend and he came with us and helped us get dope. We dropped him off. That kid gave me bad vibes and I didn't want him at my place. I had a needle at my place. We all shared that one. Nothing too eventful happened that night. I remember it was cold. Angela passed out and I thought I should call the ambulance but I shook her for a few seconds and she woke up. We went on a drive with the windows down so she would wake up a little more. She was perfectly normal when we went back to my place. It must have been close to 8:30 p.m. because we started to get our things together. She had to be home at nine. I went back to her place with her and I was having to walk home. I walked up to her room and helped her into bed. I kissed her and walked out. I told her I loved her and I didn't hear a response by the time I got to the top of the stairs. I turned around, opened her door, and said, "I love you" again. She told me she loved me. I'm glad I went back. That was the last time I heard her voice.

That night I couldn't sleep. I tried to drink myself to sleep but I stayed sober. I've never been so restless, not even through withdrawals. Angela was supposed to pick me up and I was going to take her to breakfast before she went to school. At 6 a.m. I heard knocking on my door. I opened it. It was Angela's mom's boyfriend's son. He told me Angela was in the hospital. I honestly had no idea why when he told me. Not until he started asking me what she took. I got to the hospital and was ambushed by a police officer asking me a lot of questions. He was going a mile a minute. He found someone else to ask questions. I knew it was serious then. They let us in to see Angela and told us she died. My mind was blown. Absolutely blown. At 19 it is impossible to fathom the death of someone you love. One of your friends. Angela was on a hospital bed. Discolored. I cried a lot. I looked at Bonnie and I wanted to die. Right there on the floor. I held Angela's hand. I kissed her on the cheek. I wanted to get the hell out of there. That was the last time I saw Angela.

I ended up getting arrested that day for bail jumping. I was on bail for a possession ticket I got a month earlier. I sat for a month. I missed Angela's funeral. I got accepted to a rehab center and they gave me some funding for the program. I got bailed out the day before Christmas and headed to Minnesota.

Rehab was difficult. Angela's death broke me. They wanted to hear all about it so I told them. The place I was, was a great foundation for me. They set me up with a lot of really supporting people. I learned a lot about myself. This was also the point where I realized I wanted a relationship with my family. After I left the rehab place I went to an extended care facility in Long Beach, California. It was fine. The people there rubbed me the wrong way but I still wanted to be clean. Rehab is difficult because you have to accept that basically your strategy for life was completely wrong and you must now start over. It's a mind game you must play with yourself.

After treatment I moved in with Bonnie. This point in my early sobriety was probably the most important. Bonnie took very good care of me. Once again more than I deserved. She wanted to talk about Angela as much as I did. Although I couldn't bring myself to be completely honest about everything that happened that night. I told her all I could and hated myself for not telling her the rest. I told her the whole story but kept out the part where I put the needle in Angela's arm and the fact that it was my needle.

Bonnie helped me out a lot. I hope maybe I helped her. I still feel like I owe her everything. She was a good support for me. She helped me get on my feet. Every day that she would ask me about what happened I died a little inside. She didn't do anything but she was tortured and I couldn't muster the balls to help her.

I struggled to get sober. I relapsed on other drugs besides heroin after Angela died. Before I came to prison I seemed to be on the easy road. Sobriety was coming easy. I had a job, a car, and a drive to get myself on track. I still felt hollow because I was still lying to everyone. When I was charged with reckless homicide I ended up pleading guilty to reckless homicide to avoid deferral charges. Before my sentencing I wanted to tell Bonnie about that night. I don't think I was telling her anything she didn't know in her heart. But I think we both felt a little better. That's one of those things that I'm not sure how I will be able to forgive myself for. How do you let the one person you love, your first love, die? I did. Then I lied. Bonnie said she forgives me. Maybe one day I'll be able to do that for myself.[16]

At the time of the writing of this book, Brian, Lon, and Lily were teens in high school and doing well. Carol, an adult, is on oxygen twenty-four hours a day but no longer smokes. Tim is facing a possible liver

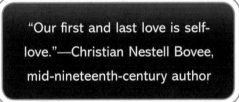

"Our first and last love is self-love."—Christian Nestell Bovee, mid-nineteenth-century author

transplant and gave this interview while he was in the hospital. Jessica has been drug and alcohol free for almost a year. Princess Peach was released from jail, and after the relapse she mentioned, had to go back and was being sentenced to prison. Brady and Kyle shared their stories while they were in jail, and then they moved on to prison. Arturo wrote his story and sent it from prison. Angela, as you know, died. Her mother met with me and shared her story.

Closing This Chapter

After reading this chapter you may have come to the realization that for as many problems out there that are related to drugs, there are solutions and many perspectives. It is important to keep searching until a solution is found. Never give up. Always keep searching and trying.

A Perspective Worth Noting

At the time this book was ready to go to press, there were still many differing opinions on how substance abuse should be dealt with. One approach is based on an effort to reduce harm to those associated with substance abuse and use, and is called harm reduction. Let's read some information from Harm Reduction International.

> Harm reduction refers to policies, programmes and practices that aim to reduce the harms associated with the use of psychoactive drugs in people unable or unwilling to stop. The defining features are the focus on the prevention of harm, rather than on the prevention of drug use itself, and the focus on people who continue to use drugs. . . .
>
> Harm reduction complements approaches that seek to prevent or reduce the overall level of drug consumption. . . . Readers can refer to Harm Reduction International website—www.ihra.net—for more detailed guidance on harm reduction interventions.[17]

Notes

1. Ryan R. Byrne, MD, assistant professor at the Medical College of Wisconsin and child and adolescent psychiatrist at Children's Hospital of Wisconsin, written for the book, 2012.
2. Chris Prentiss, *Zen and the Art of Happiness* (Los Angeles: Power Press, 2006).
3. Prentiss, *Zen and the Art of Happiness*
4. National Institute on Drug Abuse (NIDA), "Principles of Drug Addiction Treatment: A Research-Based Guide (Third Edition)," last updated December 2012, www.drugabuse.gov/publications/principles-drug-addiction-treatment-research-based-guide-third-edition/principles-effective-treatment.
5. NIDA, "DrugFacts: Treatment Approaches for Drug Addiction," revised September 2009, www.drugabuse.gov/publications/drugfacts/treatment-approaches-drug-addiction.
6. NIDA, "DrugFacts: Treatment Approaches for Drug Addiction."
7. NIDA, "DrugFacts: Treatment Approaches for Drug Addiction."
8. One Little Angel.com, "Mystics, Saints & Poets," www.onelittleangel.com/wisdom/quotes/hinduism.asp#author.
9. Yvonne Dennis, a social worker and author of more than ten books, written contribution and phone interview, January 2013.
10. NIDA, "DrugFacts: Treatment Approaches for Drug Addiction."
11. Carol was an adult at the time of her written contribution, 2012.
12. Tim was an adult at the time of the phone interview, 2012.
13. Princess Peach was no longer in high school at the time of her contribution, written contribution and interview, 2012.
14. Jessica was a young adult at the time of her phone interview, 2012.
15. Angela's story and her writing was shared by her mom, Bonnie, in an interview in 2012.
16. Arturo shared his story in a written contribution, 2012.
17. http://www.ihra.net/what-is-harm-reduction, accessed spring 2013.

HOLISTIC METHODS

"Do not follow where the path may lead. Go instead where there is no path and leave a trail."—Ralph Waldo Emerson, American essayist, lecturer, and poet

Many people feel the right path for them is to choose that which is most natural. Holistic methods are those that encourage the mind/body/spirit to work together. You'll see in this chapter that there are a lot of methods and practices and therapies that fall under the "holistic" title and most talk about "bringing together" or "connecting" instead of separating. Connecting mind, body, and breath. Connecting outside nature with inner nature. It all seems to be about connecting.

There is some fascinating stuff here, much backed by scientific fact. Read on and consider these methods for well-being. Even if you don't have a substance abuse issue, these methods and modalities can enhance your well-being! Jessica, one of the teens you have been reading about at the end of each chapter, has shared her viewpoints on holistic treatments and therapies.

In an interview with Jessica, she said,

All of these treatments are ancient, and they are still happening today. So there has got to be something that is working with them, otherwise they would have disintegrated years ago. In today's society, especially in the western hemisphere, we are so immediate; we take a pill for everything. Everything is on our time as opposed to a higher power's time. There is something to be said of time as a healer. Holistic therapy isn't a quick fix. Therapy is a long fix. Just as if you are in a car accident and you have to go to physical therapy that is so you can walk for the rest of your life, and every day you work every day you get better . . . it is the same with emotional therapy. You are reprogramming your emotions and the tools and the way you protect yourself and the way you let yourself open. You are working with therapy to be able to feel again, to be able to have some sense of normalcy to your feelings and actions and habits. So these therapies, once again, you are choosing to get better, instead of depending on a substance. These therapies engage you to engage yourself.[1]

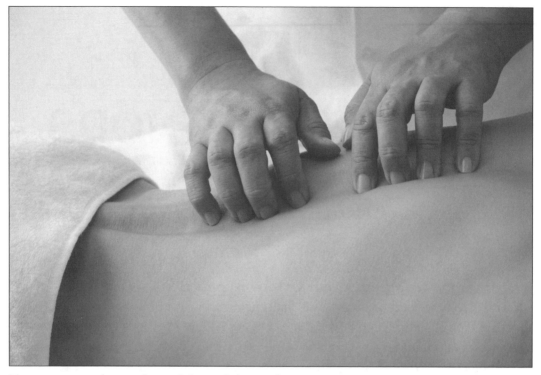

Massage can reduce pain, anxiety, and depression.

Natural High . . . No Lie![2]

Research shows that massage, a therapy practiced for thousands of years, can organically stimulate the brain to produce the very *same* chemicals that addictive substances do: *dopamine, serotonin, and endorphins.* Studies at Touch Research Institute (TRI) in Florida indicate that a regular program of massage therapy safely generates a lasting and reasonable increase in the blood levels of dopamine by 31%, serotonin by 28%, and endorphins by 16%. These are the truly "golden" chemicals that the body and brain seek in order to get "high." These natural bio-chemicals are ushered into our body *by* our body and are the vital ingredients of the true euphoria, brain-craving, and pain-free state that drives us back again and again to the addictive substance.

Massage provides the opportunity to experience those same feelings and sensations of these golden chemicals at a sustainable, healthy level without drinking, snorting, injecting, or inhaling anything but a normal breath. During all phases of addiction, massage can be a secure and reliable substitute that can quickly relieve cravings by naturally releasing those *same* chemicals into our bloodstream, though not necessarily of the same intensity. Feeling *good* while sober restores confidence in the self and trust in others through the experience of true compassion and total relaxation. It can also help to recalibrate the levels of these golden chemicals that our body and brain are craving back to an essential, inborn proportion. Massage reminds us that we can feel great sober; and it's a safe and natural way to get high . . . no lie!

Massage Reduces Anxiety, Depression, and Pain

Massage also deals with and reduces anxiety, depression, and pain. Anxiety is really just "fear" with a few more syllables. Rational fear is a normal reaction to the belief that our safety or survival may be threatened—the so-called "fight or flight" reaction. In many cases, however, the genesis of the threat is an irrational distortion by our subconscious, and if we are operating from a "disconnected" mind, body, and social environment, the fear can escalate—and often remain—far beyond normal thresholds; even becoming our reality. Anxiety can lead to depression, or vice versa, but either of these uninvited guests incites the body to produce cortisol, often called the stress hormone, which in turn, produces more anxiety and depression. Like green veggies to a child, your mind will do what it can to avoid this "bad taste" and reach for whatever it may have tasted before that instead released endorphins and dopamine that have a much "sweeter" taste than anxiety, depression, or pain.

Fortunately, massage lowers cortisol. TRI[3] (Touch Research Institute) reports that touch therapies can reduce cortisol as much as 31%, thereby breaking or reducing the loop of anxiety and depression. According to a pubmed.gov abstract,[4] massage also reduces blood pressure, which in turn, can lessen anxiety and physical discomforts of headache, dizziness, or palpitations in the chest. By decreasing tension in the muscles and increasing dopamine levels, massage reduces or eliminates pain and often helps improve sleep and increase overall energy. Body aches and sleeplessness are big problems that not only lead to and then maintain addiction, but also hinder the success of recovery during all phases. By diminishing pain, both physically and emotionally, massage is a safe, drug-free therapy for all phases of addiction.

The very nature and experience of massage facilitates a truthful, peaceful connection between the mind, body, and spirit. Since it is based purely on our own unfiltered, biological sensations of well-being, massage brings our mind and thoughts on-line and in-line with each other. In another way, it's like the body's voice becomes a recognizable source of information to the mind; for some, we become "aware" and "know" what is truly good or not good for our body and therefore better for our mind. Massage introduces a reliable internal link for us to identify and become familiar with our "Self," which can help to serve as a useful filter to weed out harmful information or thoughts that may come from an external force. This is a safer, more reliable practice whereby the possibility that "normal" exists outside the rut of addiction becomes apparent and, hopefully, will aid in the need for the addictive substance to evaporate. The vital life forces inside each of us become available as concentration and focus improves; anxiety, depression, and pain are reduced; and mind, body, and spirit meet in a true, healthy place.

Ben Benjamin, PhD in sports medicine and author of *Listen to Your Pain*, writes about the unfortunate reality that babies, deprived of human touch, are developmentally delayed or inhibited . . . some of them will actually die. This news is included here not to make the reader sad or fearful, but to demonstrate the magnitude and importance of the healing, human touch. The effects of caring, nurturing touch extend to all levels of the mind and body; much further and deeper than any foreign substance . . . *no lie!!*

Massage: An Ancient High

Jessica, who experienced massage as a teen, shares in an interview, "Massage is therapeutic in that it feels like someone is literally pulling the junk off of you and throwing it away."

Barrie Springhetti, a licensed massage therapist who, at the time this book was published, had been practicing for more than twelve years, writes about the benefits that she sees in massage (see "Natural High . . . No Lie," page 96) as well as somatics and aromatherapy. Having taught neuromuscular, massage, and aromatherapies, she has seen the outcomes firsthand.

Table 6.1 Benefits of Massage Therapy

IMPROVES/ENHANCES:	ALLEVIATES/REDUCES:
Energy	Anxiety
Circulation—blood	Depression
Detoxification	Blood pressure
Circulation—lymph	Pain
Sleep	Body aches
Relaxation	Muscle tension
Digestion	Headaches
Dopamine/Endorphins	Cortisol
Immune system	Head—static or noise
Trust—self and others	
Connects mind and body	

Table 6.1 shows many other direct and indirect advantages that massage can offer to the processes of addiction.

Aromatherapy

Aromatherapy is a type of therapy, practiced for thousands of years, which utilizes the vital fluid of plants and herbs to effect a change, either by exciting a response from or moderating an excess in all areas of mental, emotional, and physical health. The essential oil[5] of a plant has nearly all the same properties and functions as the blood that runs through our bodies; it protects the plant from bacteria, viruses, and fungi; it circulates vital nutrients throughout the plant structure; it heals wounds; and it removes wastes.

> "Essential oils make me feel relaxed when I diffuse it in my room."—Whitnie B., age 16

As a form of alternative medicine, aromatherapy is administered through inhalation or it can be applied topically to the skin or ingested for therapeutic benefits. It is important, however, that pharmaceutical-grade essential oils be used for the safest treatment protocols and results. When substandard products are used, the results may be weakened or could possibly be harmful to the person using them. It is recommended to seek the advice of an aromatherapist knowledgeable in the use of essential oils.

Similar to the functions of our own blood, the essential oil of a plant aids in the vital processes of circulation, nutrition, immunity, and overall physical health. Each of the oils has its own signature or frequency, and our bodies resonate with and tolerate these organic molecules on a profound cellular and chemical basis. Since the oils are lightweight and volatile, they easily move through the air, and the effect is easy and immediate through inhalation. Via the channel of smell, the oils are introduced directly into the limbic system of the brain, which is considered the seat of emotions, behaviors, and learned memories. The chemical signature of the ingredients that make up these essential oils are familiar to and friendly with nearly every cell in our bodies, and they can freely circulate throughout the body, including the brain and spinal cord. The oils work to naturally restore and balance the chemistry of your body and brain. They may quiet overly excited conditions as well as raise lowered capacity where needed; it's as if they are attuned to the body's needs. Many of the oils activate the body to release healthy, sustainable levels of dopamine, serotonin, endorphins, and other inborn, organic chemicals for an honest, overall sense of well-being.

Research shows that the oils infiltrate the body and act as quickly as 1/100 of a second; hence, they can instantly temper the intensity of cravings, headaches, mood swings, and many other conditions during early or sustained abstinence. Since essential oils are allowed past the blood-brain barrier and can directly affect the cellular terrain of hormones and neurotransmitters, they are very effective in reducing anxiety, depression, insomnia, and pain, as well as dramatically improving mental and cognitive clarity. Circulation and digestion are two other critical systems that benefit greatly from the use of therapeutic essential oils.[6]

Somatics

Have you ever wondered how fast your cryptic text message travels through time? The scientists tell us that LOL moves as fast as the light coming from the sun. Why then, if the data of your text travels about one billion feet per second, do you have to wait so many seconds, even minutes, for a response? Generally, it's the fiber-optic highways and software bogged down by an overloaded server . . . Wait. Stop reading this. Close your eyes. Describe in detail the experience of waking up this morning. Can you do it? Of course you can. You opened your eyes. You yawned. You pulled back the covers and dropped your feet to the floor. You walked away from your bed, and . . . okay, you can recall the mechanical, linear actions. Try now, instead, to *describe* the experience. What was it like the second before your eyelids rolled up? When they did, how did the light hit them? What smell came to you first thing in the morning? Did the fabric of your pants leave an impression on your knees? Like what? Was your jaw clenched as your thoughts swam back into the dreams you just left? Were you peaceful, nervous, confident, or dissatisfied with your thoughts? And hang on here, no fair guessing or using past experiences to write this experience. How did you really experience it *this* morning? Chances are you didn't really experience that moment fully this morning at all. Why not?

To truly experience that answer, you should reflect on the paradox of that highly accelerated text message that seems to get lost in space for a while. Your brain, body, and millions of neural pathways imitate the same text-messaging process. Imagine your mind and body costarring as the two phones relaying texts between them and the fiber optics are played by your neural pathways. Great. Right? Not right; we need to add a server to the stage or the data will never be processed. Here's where we introduce the lead role in this drama: the soma. The what? Never heard of it? You can't touch it, draw it, or see it under a microscope. Neither mind nor body, the soma is like the body's consciousness combined with the mind's personality. Huh? Think about it, it's the em*bodi*ment of the mind.

Without it, the text messages have no meaning. They are just letters dangling in space like your legs off your bed in the morning that you can't even consciously remember. The text may get to its destination, but it may or may not make sense. When we move around without somatic awareness, the two devices transmitting data, mind and body, do not have a reliable connection. The pertinent data such as interpretation of our environment, likes, dislikes, behaviors, and relationships can become contaminated or imaginary. The mind and body then function independently of one another with insufficient data, and the natural balance and rhythm of our wellness has gone astray. As you can quickly imagine, this is a perfect place for harmful behaviors and physiological habits to seed, germinate, and thrive. The stage is set for addiction to develop without intention or awareness. The reconnect of mind and body via a conscious practice of knowing and moving (with the soma) is somatics.

Somatics is a type of therapy that is rooted in a holistic, body-centered model of health and well-being. It uses the link between awareness, the body's functions, and the environment to join together (integrate) and normalize (regulate) the Self by bringing a sharp awareness to otherwise new or unknown (subtle) physical movements intended to then transmit that experience to and through a healthy mind-body connection. This field of therapy contains many distinct disciplines, each with its own therapeutic technique and approach, but the intention of revitalizing and restoring balance to the physical body through movement patterns directed from awareness of a conscious mind, is constant through all forms of somatics.[7]

Somatics can be a very helpful tool during all phases of addiction recovery. As indicated earlier, there is often a critical disconnect between the body and mind during addiction, and somatics provides safe and simple movements or sequences that can reintroduce the body to its governing principle, the mind.

Substance use is a familiar example of the body functioning without conscious awareness and connection to the mind, and it is most certainly unsafe. Addiction relies on and thrives in that disconnect, which is unsafe. Somatics gives the recovering addict an opportunity to reconnect the mind, body, and environment and function better without the substance.

Peering directly into the eyes of the mind can often prove to be unmanageable and unimaginable for the addict prior to or during recovery. The stillness can be deafening and the images not appealing. By summoning the body's personality, or soma, somatics uses the mind as an ally or counselor to fully integrate the whole body and all its systems into the complete consciousness of the mind. Once the connection is made, there is a constant, reliable conduit to the true Self. This type of conscious awareness is more vital than the kind of dependency of the addiction. Somatics is a practice rather than a technique. It is self-balancing rather than a therapy imposed by a practitioner. The practitioner is a guide that can help facilitate a safe, holistic path to the true Self that is separate and without need of addiction.[8]

Integrative Medicine

Integrative medicine is a compassionate approach using functional and metabolic testing to accurately assess individual causes of chronic illness. It combines behavioral and educational interventions along with nutrients, natural remedies, and pharmacological medications, if needed, to support restoration of healthy

Chiropractic Treatment

Dr. Karl Lickteig, a chiropractor who owns Lickteig Chiropractic and Clinic SC, shares his thoughts on this treatment:

> With a career in providing rehabilitative services by chiropractic means of treatment for twenty-five years, I have observed an ever increasing debilitation of our American population. This is unfortunate in light of the advanced medical technology of the twenty-first century in which we live. In addition to the decline of overall health in this land of abundance are degenerative processes that accompany with inflammatory tissue/diseases. These changes stem from dietary choices, stress, hastening of the farming process, genetic engineering of foodstuffs, and of course, genetics.
>
> With the ever quickening of societal demands and the subsequent barrage of data to our senses, dietary choices are often left behind. Unfortunately, these choices often constitute processed foods. Chronic use of these unnatural foods can lead to inflammatory changes at the cellular level, depressed immune response, and organ dysfunction; e.g., gastrointestinal [GI] dysbiosis (when the good bacteria is killed), adrenal fatigue, etc. Stressful situations, which we all encounter, can accelerate immune system deterioration and also lead to inflammatory changes and

their cascading effects. It is well known that the immune system controls the way our bodies manage the inflammatory process. Should there be GI dysbiosis, the immune system is consequently under attack and therefore, inflammation will result. Chronic tissue inflammation may lead to organic interruption and system failure.

The medical industry, with all its advances, will typically view the symptom before the causation. With a great deal of knowledge about pharmaceuticals, the medical practitioner will typically prescribe the requisite medication to down-regulate the symptom as opposed to initiating protocols to effect a change relative to causation. There is a time and place for said medications, however the totality of the working system requires evaluation versus only that of the symptom.

The health care model of chiropractic has long held the belief in working with the total individual. If the human system is in good functioning order, the body can manage billions of daily processes without interruption. That is barring a traumatic event of course. If we take care of our bodies, getting necessary measures of rest, recreation/conditioning, spiritual centeredness and input of good fuels/foods, we can stay ahead of degenerative and inflammatory changes. The chiropractic care model offers the body additional input by means of a well-functioning nervous system. The nervous system controls of all levels of interaction in our bodies, particularly with how the immune system functions, and the vital elements of organic control. The nervous system is involved from a musculo-skeletal perspective as well.

From an anecdotal standpoint, I have evaluated thousands of patients in my twenty-five-year chiropractic practice and noted substantial improvements relative to immune system function, inflammatory reduction at all levels and a much greater ability to respond to daily life stressors so implicated in said degenerative processes. Using the chiropractic treatment model as a resource, as well as its many assests by addressing the totality of the individual versus symptom response management, can in effect allow for a more harmonious life experience without unnecessary dis-engagement often due to accelerated degenerative changes.[9]

physiology. The doctor will also assess toxic burden and environmental expo-
sures and sensitivities to create targeted detoxification protocols.

A doctor of integrated medicine, Dr. Norm Schwartz, in practice for twenty-
one years when this book was published, states, "My goal is to work with patients
as a partner to invoke their innate human healing response. I use a multidisci-
plinary, systems approach, combining the art and science of medicine. I prescribe
natural therapies including: lifestyle changes, mind-body interventions, detoxification, nutritional and herbal remedies, hormonal and environmental assessments
to promote healing."[10]

Yoga

While the benefits of yoga for overall health have become more well known in the
West, many are now appreciating the positive effects it has on those with a substance abuse problem. Some studies have indicated that practicing yoga increases
the levels of GABA in the brain. GABA is the major inhibitory neurotransmitter, which means that it slows down the actions of the neurons. GABA acts like
brakes on a bike. Some research indicates that one of the factors in those who
have anxiety disorders or panic attacks as well as those with substance addiction
or dependence issues is low GABA activity.[11] This increase of GABA is said to be
more than 20 percent for those who engage in yoga practice regularly.

Yoga also nurtures the body, mind, and spirit at the same time, encouraging a
person's whole Self to focus on well-being. Yoga can help people release, not just
muscle tension, but also emotional tension. While our bodies are made to be able
to eliminate toxins through a variety of methods, when our systems are stressed,
yoga can assist by helping get rid of toxins from different organs. Yoga helps the
person come to know his or her true nature through a mindful practice that encourages the person to become aware of his or her body, thoughts, and breath.
Yoga helps people in some ways that are in line with the twelve-step program,
such as fostering acceptance. Addiction is known as a disease that separates, not
only people from people through destructive relationships, but the destruction
that occurs within a person's own self. The mind and body are at odds with each
other in an addiction, and often the spiritual component is nowhere to be found.
Yoga is the opposite. Yoga unifies body, mind, and breath/spirit so that the Self
can work as a whole to reach its unlimited potential. When the Self is in balance,
outside relationships can be nurtured.

Pranayama is the practice of controlled breathing, often done within the practice of yoga, and is often referred to as the art of yoga breathing. Breathing is one
of the most vital functions of life, and pranayama promotes proper breathing,
which is to bring control of Prana (the vital life energy). Combining asana (yoga

Remember to Breathe

Jessica talks about her experiences with yoga:

> What I like about yoga is that it is self-healing. It incorporates meditation with movement and breathing. Before, as addicts, we engaged in self-destructive behavior. This is self-constructive behavior, we are doing this to ourselves. In yoga you are not only exercising your breath and muscles and working on posture, but also exercising your willpower and decision making, and that is the therapy we need. We need decision-making therapy. Before I go into a yoga class, always, always, there is anxiety for me. I have a huge fear of being imperfect and when I am in class I worry I am going to fall on my face, or I'm going to mess up or I'm not going to do it right or I'm going to disappoint. In actuality, what I've come to realize is that just being there is being it perfectly. During the class I have something to focus on. Yoga is like a mental pacifier, and so my anxiety goes away. When class ends I try to take everything I've done in class which is now freshly in me, and I do my best to carry that throughout my day and to remember to breathe and be gentle and kind and forgiving. With myself first and then with others. It's hard, but that's the idea.[12]

poses) with pranayama as well as meditation covers mind and body and spirit, and fosters self-discipline and purification.[13] Have you ever felt really stressed about something? Maybe an exam, or having to give a speech in front of a class? Even walking into a party can make some people really anxious. Learning breathing methods can help regulate the "fight or flight" mode your body moves into, helping you to relax and be calm. Ahhhh . . .

Meditation

Meditation, like the other methods and practices, can enhance well-being for those dealing with substance use disorders as well as those without. Meditation, often a part of yoga classes and a part of traditional practice, can increase peace of mind, enhance spirituality, decrease stress, and help a person release tension, and therefore, it can also be an important part of a person's recovery plan. People wanting to know about meditation can read about it, hire a trained professional, find a teacher, and practice on their own.

Meditation can help people become more aware and see things from a different perspective, allowing them to gain a better understanding of what may be contributing to their substance abuse.

Meditation can enhance the feeling of calmness, but often, when the practice becomes more regular, this new state of awareness and peace can extend beyond the meditation sessions. This can come about in part because the meditator gains access to internal awareness that allows the person to be less reactive. Have you ever felt embarrassed about the way you reacted in a certain situation? Maybe you lost your temper or said things you wish you wouldn't have? Meditation can help you gain control of your thoughts.

Here is something pretty cool: "A Harvard psychologist named Richard Davidson has done brain scans on dozens of Buddhist monks and found that their training has permanently altered their limbic systems, giving them heightened empathy—or the ability to understand and identify with another person's feelings."[14] In the article, Eric Wargo mentions that another researcher from Harvard discovered that training for eight weeks in methods like mindfulness, meditation, and yoga increased the gray matter in the areas of the brain that have to do with motor control, breathing, emotion, learning, and memory. Do you recall what part of the brain develops last? Do you recall how drugs affect the brain negatively?

These findings help show that this holistic stuff you are reading about here isn't just fluff. There are studies that show these practices make a difference. Sometimes when teens are faced with all of the changes going on in their bodies (like hormones) and all the stresses they are faced with, it may seem there is little that can help make teens feel balanced, at ease, and calm. Sadly, these are often the times teens turn to chemical substances. Knowing about these holistic methods, and that they can actually work, can help!

Exercise

It is obvious that exercise is good for people (as long as there aren't underlying health issues that could complicate the condition) and that it is better for your bod to be outside playing tennis

"When I'm feeling stressed out from too much homework or something, I'll go for a run. It relaxes me and makes me feel healthy."—Kaiti B., age 14

rather than inside watching television. You can probably share your own experiences about how good you feel after you've played tag with your little sister and how sluggish and gross you feel after you've watched a marathon day of television episodes while indulging on chips. But how does exercise affect treatment for substance abuse issues?

Exercise can help both physically and emotionally during recovery. Exercise can release endorphins (remember, that natural high), and it can relieve stress and tension as well.[15] Having a strong body that is physically fit through exercise can aid in healing, including the healing of substance abuse disorders.

Eat Well to Be Well

Eating "right" can be a tricky thing. After all, what is "right"? There are all kinds of right ways of eating, depending upon the resources you read. You can eat no meat, you can eat practically all meat; you can cut out gluten or carbs, eat a diet of high or low carbs, eat only raw food, and eat organically.

Probably everyone agrees it's best to eat a balanced diet. Eating foods from the earth, like fruits, veggies, nuts, and grains, is an important way to get your vitamins and minerals. Many researchers are saying that eating organic foods (foods that haven't been sprayed with toxins) is the way to go. But make no mistake about it, eating healthy is a critical part of being healthy. And it is also a critical part of the process of recovery for someone dealing with substance abuse disorders.

According to Alcoholics Victorious, "In order to help people recover, it is important to understand the impact of nutrition. It is astounding to consider that only fat contains more calories per gram than alcohol. As a result, while drinking, addicts experience a sense of fullness having eaten very little or nothing. These 'empty calories' lead to poor eating habits and malnutrition. Drug abusers experience a similar affect. Alcohol and drugs actually keep the body from properly absorbing and breaking down nutrients and expelling toxins. This leads to a host of health problems."[16]

So, don't dismiss the notion of "you are what you eat." If you eat healthier, you will be healthier.

It's a Fact!

Alcoholics Victorious also states, "Nutrition actually impacts cravings for drugs and alcohol. Every newly recovering addict struggles with craving to use alcohol and drugs. Research has shown that a diet with the right types of high protein and high carbohydrate-rich foods can make a big difference."[17]

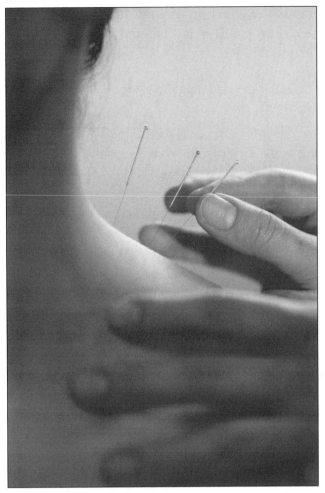

Acupuncture can help with sleep issues, pain, anxiety, and more.

Acupuncture

Jessica has enjoyed the benefits of acupuncture. She shares in an interview, "I am a huge advocate for acupuncture. The needles don't feel like needles. It isn't like you are getting a shot or taking blood, it is like you are being touched from the inside out in places where you hold tension and emotional stress. It is like releasing air in a tire slowly, lowering the emotional pressure."[18]

Jori Azinger is a licensed acupuncturist and feels that this type of therapy has a place in the treatment of addiction. She writes,

Lots of people kinda freak out when they hear acupuncture and lots and lots of people are finding out that receiving acupuncture care can shift a lot. It's not usually a quick fix. However, it can be a permanent one.

Acupuncture is the insertion of solid stainless steel, hair-thin needles through the skin. It is painless and blissful for most folks. After an initial meeting, evaluation and looking at your tongue, doing 12 pulses on both wrists and palpating your abdomen you are ready for your first treatment. You get to lie down and close your eyes (or watch if you like) and relax. Most of my clients quickly express how surprised they are that it doesn't hurt and many fall into one of the most peaceful sleeps they've experienced in a long time. Resting in what I call the bliss abyss for about 30 minutes feels like about two minutes.

Detox can be pretty rough; anything you can do to help yourself needs to be your top priority. Whatever your detox symptoms are acupuncture can help with them. Sleep issues, pain, overwhelming anxiety and on and on. If you have been struggling, especially without any support, you need to find some people to help you. There are many caring practitioners that can help. Acupuncture is a fantastic way to help yourself through any physical, emotional, mental or spiritual log jams in your systems. It can help you feel better and help you stay motived to continue helping yourself into a life with possibility, opportunity and joy. Imagine that! No really! Imagine that! NOW GO FOR IT![19]

Reiki

Jessica shares, "Reiki is an incredible feeling, you actually feel like your body is humming."[20]

Reiki is a well-being technique that enhances stress reduction and relaxes the client. It can also promote healing. The Japanese technique is an idea based on keeping the life force energy flowing by releasing energy blocks. A Reiki practitioner lays his or her hands on or near the client, who is fully clothed and usually lying down. How does it feel to receive Reiki? Some teens have described it as a feeling of heat where the Reiki master's hands are hovering. Others feel coolness. Still others experience a buzzing. Most feel a sense of calmness and relaxation that lasts even after the session ends. Reiki has been used in recovery centers, and some stats indicate that it has shown to help with clarity and sobriety. It can help in the withdrawal process as well.

The Arts and Creative Arts Therapy

You've experienced some form of art before, right? Gone to a play or been in one? Listened to music or sang a song? Seen a painting or drawn a picture? The arts

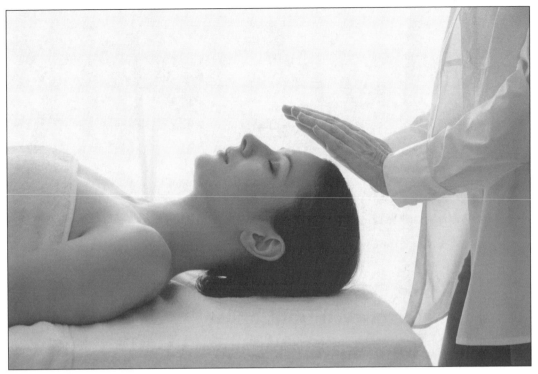

Reiki is a well-being technique that enhances stress reduction and relaxes the client.

have long been a part of history and culture and for good reason. The arts are a way for people to connect with others because art is a universal language.

But there's more; being involved in the process of creating is invaluable as well—to express, be creative, imagine, and communicate in ways that can cross language barriers while getting people in touch with their passions and inner Self. As a therapy the focus is less on the end result (like a story, play, poem, or song) but more on the process (like acting, singing, writing, or drawing).

Some of the therapies are dance, art, drama, writing, and music. But there are more ways to express oneself, such as photography, yoga, and needlework. Through these expressions, the artist can get to know him- or herself better because often the act of creating is a letting go. It is driven by feelings and emotions, and through this process, the person can come in touch with emotions that could have, up until then, been buried.

Art and art therapy can reduce stress and improve self-esteem because they give the individual a focus and a sense of accomplishment. They can help people express feelings that they might not verbally be able to (perhaps because they can't put it into words or perhaps they haven't even accessed these feelings). All of this can enhance treatment for substance abuse, including the effectiveness of working with a therapist, who can analyze the drawing or sculpture, which may

Visual Arts

Paula Christensen, the visual arts director of North Shore Academy of the Arts, Inc., the Arts Mill, and an artist, wrote,

> When I was a teen I knew finding the correct words to say to another teen could be intimidating. Often it left me feeling inadequate and frustrated by not saying what I really meant to say. Then I discovered expression in art. The act of self-expression is valuable. To me as a teen it was priceless. On a canvas, a piece of paper, or in a clump of clay I could gently draw what I meant or by contrast aggressively carving the clay and the meaning. The movement mimicking the emotion. The inability to express these emotions can be repressive. Not only is the action of art helpful but also the spiritual connection to what I was trying to say in the art. Often as a teen you feel no one wants to listen to you. Yet in an art room everyone wants to listen. The creation of art is the history of storytelling. Within the boundaries of creation comes an endless source of self-expression and freedom no matter how mainstream or not. To repress your creativity is to repress your history. I spent most of my high school years in the art room. My teachers were welcoming and encouraging. It was there I found my words. Because of that I continue to create and feel the need to pay it forward and work with teens. Many of my students now work side by side with me. Creating and sharing one language.[21]

help a person address issues that might have contributed to his or her substance use and abuse.[22]

Performing arts can be in the form of plays, musicals, dance. It can be a song sung on stage, a pantomime, a puppet show, a band, a flutist, a violin. It can be ballet or a movie seen on a screen. Performing arts can be enjoyable and relaxing to watch, and inspiring and healing to engage in. Like other forms of art, it can build self-esteem and help the participants feel a part of a community or help them discover truths about themselves.[23]

Performing Arts

Angela Mack, vocal director and director for North Shore Academy of the Arts, Inc., and musician, wrote about her experiences with music,

> One of the supreme joys that I have as a music director and teacher is to see and know the positive influence that music has on the lives of my students. Being able to express oneself through song has its miraculous benefits. Having an avenue to release emotions through creative expression is extremely life giving to the entire well-being of an individual. In a society plagued by stress, anxiety, addiction, depression, chronic and mood disorders, and low self-esteem, music is an ancient avenue to help ease such maladies. It is a scientific fact that music releases the "feel good" neurochemical dopamine in the brain which can improve mood, help eradicate negative emotions and memories and aid in concentration. Music can be used as a means to cope and I have seen it used in profound ways in the lives of many of my students over the years.[24]

Literary Arts

Poetry, fiction, nonfiction—all are a form of art and can be beneficial to those working through issues and toward healing. Reading can be relaxing and can also share insights of a topic or experience without the reader really truly having to experience it. Often, reading can be a safe form of escape for teens (or people of any age). Writing is also a means of therapy. Many rehab programs include writing as an exercise for the patient to discover things about him- or herself that perhaps are being hidden under layers of hurt and pain. Keeping journals or diaries can be a safe way to express thoughts and emotions.

Nature

You might be saying, "Are you kidding? Now you are saying that a walk in the woods can help me get over this intense addiction?" Research says exactly that.

Arts and Self-expression

Alisa, a performing artist and director for children's musicals, said in an interview,

Group arts, like a musical production or a dance team, can be beneficial in the way that when you are busy and have to be accountable to others, and you care about what you are doing, your focus will be less on "partying" and more on your art form. How do I feel the arts are of value? It is a form of self-expression, an outlet. It is personality building and friendship building. If you want to achieve your goals in the arts, you need too much determination and too much passion to allow your focus to be diverted to drugs. It is about knowing what you want.[25]

At the Movies

Movies are a form of performing arts. The following movies are related to the topic of substance abuse:

The Basketball Diaries, 1995. This movie is about a young basketball player who falls into drugs.

Boyz in the Hood, 1991. This movie is a coming-of-age story about growing up in black urban America.

City of God, 2002. Two boys growing up in a violent neighborhood of Rio de Janeiro take different paths and one becomes a drug dealer.

Dazed and Confused, 1993. The adventures of incoming high school and junior high students on the last day of school involve the use of drugs.

Thirteen, 2003. This movie is about a thirteen-year-old girl discovering drugs, sex, and petty crime and how it affects her relationship with her mother.

Off the Bookshelf

Here are some books that might be of interest on the topic of substance abuse.

Beautiful Boy by David Sheff, 2009. This memoir can be described as "a father's journey through his son's addiction."

Crank by Ellen Hopkins, 2004. This novel is about a loosely true story about the author's daughter's addiction with crystal meth.

Fallout by Ellen Hopkins, 2012. This novel is about the children of a mother addicted to crystal meth.

Glass by Ellen Hopkins, 2007. Kristina is back in the grips of crystal meth, even though she now has a baby to care for.

Recovery Road by Blake Nelson, 2011. This book is about a teen coming out of rehab and going back to her school where she was known as Mad Dog Maddie.

Smack by Melvin Burgess, 2010. This book is about two teenagers and heroin use.

Tweak: Growing Up on Methamphetamines by Nic Sheff, 2009. This autobiography tells the same basic story as *Beautiful Boy* but from the boy's point of view.

We All Fall Down by Nic Sheff, 2012. This book's subtitle describes the topic: "living with addiction."

Nature and a Teen

Lily, the eighth grader from the stories you read at the end of chapter 1, shares her thoughts about nature: "I go into nature when I need a break from the constant hustle and bustle of life. Just breathing in the fresh air somehow calms me down and lets me think about things that I wouldn't think about anywhere else. Seeing the beauty of the woods reminds me that there are such simple things in life that can make me happy. This gives me a sense of relief and makes me appreciate the little things more."[26]

Nature can assist in many ways for many things. Try taking some time in nature to find your own true nature. It's true, hanging out with the trees, a stream, near a mountain, even in a park can help in subtle ways that can assist in your healing. Most feel an immediate sense of release; a relief that helps make them calm and feel more peaceful.

Have you ever heard of "forest bathing," which is a method of spending time in nature to improve yourself? The practice of forest bathing is a popular practice in Japan. The Japanese word for forest bathing is *Shinrinyoku*.

It may surprise you that the brain is influenced by nature. Some studies suggest that spending time within a forest can lessen stress, depressive symptoms, and anger. It can also improve sleep and increase the feelings of having energy.

But there is more. According to research about the Japanese practice of forest bathing, spending time in nature affects not only our emotional well-being, but our physical well-being as well.

An assistant professor at Nippon Medical School in Tokyo has done research to determine how forest bathing affects our immune systems, stress levels, and moods. Some of the experiments led him to believe that forest bathing, done on a regular basis, increases natural killer cell activity. Killer cells are cells that help protect by killing abnormal cells! In addition, the practice of forest bathing can lower the chances of psychosocial stress-related diseases. Part of this could be due to breathing in wood essential oils, called phytoncides, which are given off by trees. Since we know that addictions need stress to thrive, this practice might be able to help a person on the path to becoming well from substance disorders.[27]

"What Is My Part in This?"

"All of these eastern ways of healing are not a pill and not a shot or anything like that. It has to come from a place of willingness; you have to believe in it, you have to subscribe to it. No one is making you do it. To realize the full benefits of it you have to have a subscription to the prescription. When I go get a massage or Reiki or acupuncture, I ask myself, 'What is my part in this?' It is usually to be receptive and mindful and breathing. Instead of asking just what they are doing for me, I ask what am I doing for me, how am I healing myself? How am I an open channel between this healing process and my true self?"—Jessica, in an interview for this book

More Well-Being and Healing Techniques and Modalities

In addition to what you just read, there are more areas for you to consider looking into not only to help with substance abuse recovery but to help you be well in general. These include, but aren't limited to Ayurveda, biofeedback, tai chi, sound therapy, color therapy, homeopathy, hypnosis, journaling, and Qigong.

Holistic methods offer many approaches to not only problems, but solutions and ultimately, a way to live your life.

Notes

1. Jessica shared her comments in a phone interview, 2012–2013.
2. Barrie Springhetti, LMT, written contribution, 2012.
3. Touch Research Institute, http://www.ncbi.nlm.nih.gov/ubmed/16162447.
4. See www.ncbi.nlm.nih.gov/pubmed/16494570 and www.ncbi.nlm.nih.gov/pubmed/22039381.
5. *Essential Oils Desk Reference* (n.p.: Essential Science Publishing, June 2000).
6. Barrie Springhetti, LMT, written for the book, 2012.
7. Thomas Hanna, *Somatics* (Boston: Addison-Wesley Publishing Company, 1988).
8. Barrie Springhetti, LMT, and Sheri M. Bestor, written for the book, 2012
9. Karl A. Lickteig, DC, CCSP, CCEP, written for the book, 2012.
10. Dr. Norm Schwartz, phone interview, 2012.
11. Novus Medical Detox Center. Those with substance abuse typically have lower levels of GABA.
12. Jessica was interviewed over the phone for her ideas on yoga, 2012.
13. Sheri Bestor, www.balancingartsyoga.com
14. Eric Wargo, NIDA, Office of Science Policy and Communications. "The Art of Meditation: Focusing Your Brain," http://teens.drugabuse.gov/blog/post/art-meditation-focusing-your-brain.
15. Kristine Lockwood, "Can Exercise Help Treat Addiction?" *Huffington Post,* February 22, 2012, http://www.huffingtonpost.com/2012/02/21/addiction-treatment-exercise_n_1291862.html (accessed fall 2012).
16. Alcoholics Victorious, "The Impact of Diet and Nutrition on Recovery," alcoholicsvictorious.org/faq/diet.html (accessed fall 2012).
17. Alcoholics Victorious, "The Impact of Diet and Nutrition on Recovery."
18. Jessica was an adult at the time she was interviewed about acupuncture, 2012–2013
19. Jori Azinger, L.Ac, HeartSpace, www.myheartspace.org and jori@myheartspace.org, written for the book, 2012.
20. Jessica shared her thoughts about Reiki in 2012–2013.
21. Paula DeStefanis Christensen, written contribution, 2012.
22. Lee Morgan, "Art Therapy as a Treatment for Drug Addiction," eHow, http://www.ehow.com/way_5451808_art-therapy-treatment-drug-addiction.html (accessed fall 2012).
23. North Shore Academy of the Arts, Inc., www.northshoreacademyofthearts.org.

24. Angela Mack, www.paramountshome.org, written for the book, 2012.

25. Alisa, performing artist, musical theatre director, an interview, 2012.

26 Lily, written contribution.

27. Healthy Parks, Healthy People Central, www.hphpcentral.com/.

MORE TO THINK ABOUT

"We are what we think. All that we are arises with our thoughts.
With our thoughts, we make our world."
—Buddha, spiritual teacher. Buddhism was founded on his teachings.

This chapter is about seeing a topic from different views. In this chapter you will hear from a variety of people, of all different ages, living in different areas. You'll hear about different career paths and different belief systems. But all of these people, in one way or another, have been enriched by experiences that help them to offer guidance.

So this chapter won't be just about stats and facts and scientific research. It will be about advice, opinions, thoughts, and feelings. It contains all different perspectives so that you can come to your own conclusions.

Let's begin with some advice from teens:

No one can make you do something you don't want to do, and no one will. Only you can control your body and what you do with it. You are the one [who] has to convince yourself to do what's best for your body even if it is difficult. I know it does not seem like a big deal and I get where you're coming from. I've been in your position, but just realize all the consequences that come from that sip or hit you are about to take. Nothing can make your body feel as good as what standing up for yourself feels like and doing what you believe is right.—Whitnie Bestor, age 16[1]

One line of advice is always stop and ask yourself, "How am I going to feel about myself tomorrow?" Then see if it's really worth it.—Kaiti Bestor, age 14[2]

This chapter is about seeing the topic from different views.

I think it is important that if someone asks you to do something you don't want to, that you stand up for yourself.—Hailie Bestor, age 11[3]

I think that teens need to stay busy doing something constructive. Never get started on drugs cause once you get started it will be hard to get off of them it will be a pain. Don't get started with any drugs or alcohol. It will lead to incarceration and other bad things down the road.—Kyle[4]

Think deeply about what you are about to do; don't let something control you. You have to change for yourself, then for others. If you only say you're changing to please others, you won't change. You never know how deeply something can affect your loved ones and yourself, until it happens. One lesson learned was knowing how letting a substance control you psychologically can alter your thought pattern and ruin you.—Brady[5]

My advice: Make your bed. Make your bed every morning, with intention behind it. When you make your bed in the morning, everything else becomes just a little less daunting. So for me, once I started making my bed, I was then able to pick up my room. From there I could write my rent check. One thing at a time. Now I am caught up. It takes one initial action to move down the path of well-being. Do a chore. It might not be fun, but you can make it into a meditation of sorts. Looking back what might have changed my course of becoming an addict? If only I had learned how to be present and not judge my thoughts back before I tried using. And not judge my actions but observe them. If you can change your thoughts, you can change your life. Also, consider the opposite action rule. If you are mad at your mom and want to isolate yourself in your room, go talk with her instead. Or if you get upset and want to eat ice cream, stop yourself. Eat carrots or go on a walk instead. Even if you don't want to, JUST TRY IT. If it is uncomfortable yet positive and healthy, keep pushing through. Just because a positive activity doesn't feel natural doesn't mean you shouldn't do it. You should keep practicing until it does feel natural.—Jessica.[6]

Let today be the first day of your new commitment for a new future. The past is yesterday and cannot be changed. Today is made out of decisions that we made yesterday. Today's choices will help shape tomorrow and tomorrow will be decided by actions of today. Take responsibility for your actions and decisions today. So you can shape tomorrow your way. Imagine yourself to be a new different person and then make it so.—Kyle[7]

The only advice I have not shared with you so far and to share with the world is: substance abuse is a major issue in today's society. We are constantly surrounded and subjected to these awful things that endanger us to obsessions and deadly addiction and near death or death experiences. These awful things will never go away. They unfortunately live in today's society; they creep up on us in the most unexpected ways. They find their homes next door to us in our children's bedrooms, our parents' closets, in the hands of ones closest to us. They find their way into the school system, the public places we attended. It does not matter whether you are the cheerleader on the football team or the most respected member in your community. You can even be a mother, a father, someone's son and or daughter, the most important career choice, a judge, nurse, law enforcement. Substance abuse can come in any shape or form and it can cause life-threatening problems. The best advice I can give to anyone is to know it can happen to anyone and it is a serious disease and should be treated like any other disease, cancer or a simple cut on your finger. In order to bandage this disease we need to help and support one another to fight the awful demons that merge in us addicts. We addicts cannot do it alone!—Princess Peach[8]

Thoughts Shared by Adults

> "Accept no one's definition of your life, but define yourself."
> —Harvey Fierstein, American actor and playwright

Here are some thoughts shared by adults in various professions and with various perspectives.

Childhood is the foundation on which we build the entire structure of life. A healthy and happy childhood ensures that we will grow into a healthy and happy person. The fear, anger, sadness, and loneliness we harbor during our childhood become a source of misery throughout our life. When these unpleasant emotions grip our children, quite often they get involved in substance abuse. Family circumstances and peer pressure reinforce their involvement with drugs and alcohol. Proper guidance, education, and most importantly, loving care can help our kids heal their emotional injuries and restore the joy of youthfulness.—Pandit Rajmani Tigunait, PhD, spiritual head, Himalayan Institute [9]

Be honest with yourself, and find that one person, the adult in [your] life that [you] can talk to. Be honest with that person. Goal setting is important, to think about how you can achieve your goals with and without substances.—Janet Osherow, LICSW, family services coordinator, Maryland[10]

Throughout my schooling as an undergraduate majoring in psychology, having taken classes in neuroscience, neuropsychology, and neurochemistry, to becoming a state certified Substance Abuse Counselor in Training, I have learned a great deal about drugs and society. In addition, having been a teen and having felt the need to fit in, carrying the weight of peer pressure, and wanting to break from my parents' rules has helped me to realize that regardless of the stigma placed on using drugs recreationally (i.e., drug abuse), drugs are not biased; from experimenting to chronic use (addiction) the human brain is affected.—John R. Mabry, SAC-IT[11]

What I learned is that even with all my interventions, I could not squelch her curiosity and interest in drugs. When she finally admitted that she was addicted to heroin, almost in the same breath she said, "I didn't think I'd become addicted." That's probably what every addict says. As we've come to learn, heroin is one of the most addicting drugs out there. You only need to ingest it a few times to become an addict. There is not a warning label that comes with your purchase nor is the dealer going to caution you. So let me caution you, it only takes a few times to become an addict. You, the teenagers and young adults here, spend a lot of time together. If you care about each other, we need your help in intervening and protecting each other from experimenting with these hard drugs. Parents, we need to support each other. As someone said, if we weren't so concerned about how we would be judged as parents, maybe we'd all be more open about our problems. Heroin has one of the lowest recovery rates. If Angela's death will affect just one person, who knows who she's saving—maybe the next greatest inventor, artist, musician, or author.—Bonnie, Angela's mom[12]

Seriously pause and give thought to the path they might be headed down and how it could be changing their lives forever.—Tom Frank, chief of police[13]

Listen to that tiny voice in your stomach that hardly gets heard. It is going to tell you if something is right or wrong. It can't always compete with the noise in your ears, but even if that voice is tiny, it is completely powerful.—Alisa, performing artist[14]

If you had any advice to give to a teen (a teen at any stage), what would it be?
My best advice would be that life gets better for most people after adolescence. There is a whole world of different viewpoints and cultures outside of high school. If you need help, there is always an adult who can help you, whether that be a parent, teacher, counselor, doctor, or friend's parent.
If you hoped teens would understand one thing that could help them when making choices, what would it be?
Put yourself in the shoes of yourself tomorrow and ask yourself, "Will I be happy tomorrow if I make this decision today?"
Are there any myths about addiction that you'd like to speak to?
The biggest myth that exists for substance abuse or any mental health disorder is that it is unusual or it means that there is something wrong with you. Every school has teenagers who struggle with substance abuse. A teenager who uses substances is not alone.—Ryan Byrne, MD[15]

What have I have learned from those who have struggled with issues of addiction? Why do many people start? Some may do it out of curiosity but often it is due to some longing, some trauma that has occurred in their lives that drugs become a way to fill that longing or to mask the pain. I think of a woman 70 years of age who came from a good family. She was a military brat and had lived all over the world. She began experimenting with drugs when she was 26. It was the light stuff at first but eventually it grew to the hard stuff until she finally settled on crack that she smoked until she was 68. She has now been clean for over a year. It was a process that came after she began to look deep into her life and examine the hurts. The childhood that was never there, the father who was not present emotionally and the number of bad relationships with men that she had been involved in all in an attempt to find a love that had eluded her. What I would say to young people now is you must learn to love yourself. Your dignity, your value and your self-worth are defined by God. It is intrinsic. The best gift that you can give yourself is to surround yourself with people who seek only your well-being. Seek those people out who will love you and who will love you unconditionally. And if addiction should become an issue for you, remember it is not the end of the world. Learn to forgive yourself and then commit to the work of finding healing.—Reverend Kenneth Wheeler[16]

As a doctor who has treated many people addicted to all kinds of substances, I understand why people seek refuge in drugs: when they have too much emotional pain or are bored with their lives, or if their friends urge them to join them in drug use. It's a risky road. Emotional pain needs help, not anesthetizing oneself with substances; boredom means there is a deep dissatisfaction with life—drugs can temporarily soothe it but they cannot take it away, it needs to be looked at; and friends mean well, but they don't necessarily know what's good for you. Each person needs to sort these issues out for themselves and really listen to their own gut feelings. If in doubt, you are best to seek help from any mature person that you know and trust. Finally, I don't agree with attempts to control drug use by police methods. Drug use is a human issue with psychological and physiological roots in people's life experience. Employing legal means to combat it never diminishes drug use, encourages trafficking and causes many people to suffer years in jail. The legal drugs like alcohol and cigarettes are much more dangerous to health—it makes no sense to arbitrarily allow such potentially lethal substances to be sold openly, while outlawing others. Everyone knowledgeable agrees that the War on Drugs is worse than a failure—it is the source of much misery.—Gabor Maté, MD[17]

Someone who has an addiction needs an outlet or a resource. If you don't find that, you are in trouble.—Tim, recovering alcoholic[18]

Teens Advice to Adults

I asked teens what advice they would like to give to adults. Here is what two of them said:

> Sit them down and talk to them. Don't just approach them out of nowhere then they will try to either deny or lie about how much and what they are using. Take certain steps in approaching them.—Kyle[19]

Advice from Me, to Myself

Dear Younger Me,

I am a teenager now, and I want to tell you not to worry. I know you're scared but THERE ARE NO SUCH THINGS AS MONSTERS OR BOOGIE MEN. Nothing is crawling under your bed or out of the dark closet. And they never will. You are completely safe, and you're going to be okay!

See you in a few years . . . :)

Me

Dear Teenage Me,

I hate to tell you this, but I was wrong. There ARE real monsters and they're much scarier than anything you dreamed up as a kid. They don't look at all like what you had ever imagined. In fact, they look perfectly NORMAL! You'll meet them every day and so will all of your friends. Kids are going to die because of them, athletes will lose their will or ability to compete, and some of the smartest of your peers will go to prison or be involved in violent traffic deaths and suicides because of them. Nothing that ever jumped out from a closet or crawled from beneath the bed will ever prove as scary and deadly as the monster of addiction that could entrap you the first time you take that one pill or that single drink.

Thanks for protecting me by the choices you're making now. You gave us a great life.

See you in twenty.

Me[20]

To adults and how they deal with teens:
Talk to them. Don't yell. Talk.—Brady[21]

Thinking about Your Future

Many people feel that it may help young people avoid substances if they consider the long-term goals for their life and how getting involved in substances may affect them. Honing in on your own interests and skills may inspire you to direct your energy toward your future career path—though, as you've learned, there are many other components involved when it comes to making "choices"; inspiration is one factor and perhaps hearing from adults who are involved with various careers might ignite some interest in teens. Do you have interests that you'd like to pursue that could lead to a career choice?

Obviously, all teens, including those dealing with addiction issues, have abilities, characteristics, and strengths that can be nurtured and lead to a successful means of making a living. The intention of including these comments about various careers is to help teens who are pre-substance consider long-term goals when making decisions. The statements are also for teens who are involved with substances and who are beginning to look more closely at what they hope to do with their lives as well as nurturing those strengths and interests even while recovering from an addiction. You might find hope in learning about these careers when you realize you could be and would successful at such a work choice. Being inspired, you might begin to nurture those strengths, even while recovering from an addiction. While pressures are often tremendous when it comes to grades and getting into the right college, there is a perspective that when it comes to future careers, getting "somewhere" means pursuing your interests and that which allows your inner light to shine.

So read these over, see what each person likes about his or her job and see what each believes is needed to be successful. This may be helpful when you are making decisions about what you might want to pursue as you grow out of your teen years. And maybe you'll notice that although the career paths are very different, many call for common characteristics to achieve success. In fact, you be the researcher now. When you go through these career comments, let's see if you can discover the common traits needed for each and every career choice.

Whatever your mind can conceive and believe, it can achieve.—Napoleon Hill, American author in personal success literature

For my job/career I am a business leader. Call it CEO, Group SVP, whatever the titles have been, for my career, I grow things; people, teams, busi-

There is a perspective that when it comes to future careers, getting "somewhere" means pursuing your interests and that which allows your inner light to shine.

nesses. Whether it's running a part of someone else's company, running my own, teaching, coaching youth sports, it is about making a difference, and about growing. A little or a lot. Every day. The attributes that are needed for me to succeed in this position include listening, persuasiveness, empathy, and understanding. These may seem to be, but are not, innate. They are learned, in classrooms and board rooms, on the farm or athletic field. They come down to paying attention and assessing, evaluating, applying, and learning without ceasing. The best thing about this career/job/ position is that when well done, it leaves a permanent positive imprint on the lives of others. Even when done poorly, the work I do shapes perspectives, and as in life, everyone I interact with in my career is faced with an opportunity to either like what I do and how I do it—and perhaps someday emulate it; or to dislike what I do and how I do it—and hopefully do it better for the exposure. I get to teach without getting paid like a teacher and I get to challenge the status quo without being a rabble rouser. I get to bring about change, and to see its impact in the environments I serve.

From my experience, I believe that if you want to do this job/career/ position when you grow up, you have to be willing to fail as you grow up. Try something you know you've never done. Keep trying until you can do it, or until you understand why you can't. Then find another way. Leadership isn't about the degrees you earn in school or the years you put in "on your way up the ladder." Leadership is about learning a better way, and using it to make a difference.—Steve Heston, founder and managing principal, The Heston Group, LLC[22]

I am a lawyer who specializes in appellate law. In other words, after someone loses a trial, they hire me to try to get an appellate court or even the Supreme Court to reverse the trial court's decision. My job requires excellent communication skills—both written and oral. Most of the communication with the appellate court takes place in writing so an ability to write persuasively is a must. Most cases involve oral argument as well, so the ability to make a clear, persuasive and orderly oral presentations is a must. I have the opportunity to right a wrong and help the courts set the correct rule that will govern an entire region or even the entire nation. My job allows me a lot of flexibility to work when I want to (but it does require a lot of work).

From my experience, I believe that if you want to do this job/career/ position when you grow up, you need to work hard at school and look for ways to improve your communication skills, such as participating in debate or forensics. Also read books written by people who write well and try to learn from them.—Paul, appellate attorney[23]

★★★All opinions expressed below are my own, are not official positions and do not represent policy of any branch or organization of the U.S. Navy or U.S. government.★★★

For my job/career I am a Public Affairs Officer in the United States Navy. I am a spokesperson for the Navy, and help manage our communications within the service and with the public.

The attributes that are needed for me to succeed in this position include . . . a dynamic and flexible attitude—I really never know what is going to come next. The ability to work quickly and well in stressful situations is also very important. Being a leader, and being able to work with a wide variety of people, including international partners, civilians, and members of the press is vital to doing my job well. The best thing about this career/job/position is the experience. I have been to 11 countries, and lived in 3 of them, including both coasts of the U.S. I pursued pirates on the high seas off Somalia and have seen the end of a rainbow in the Straits of Magellan. I have met Olympic athletes and movie stars (and been on set of a major motion picture). I have worked with men and women who are truly heroes, by any definition of the word, and get to work beside some of the finest people I have ever met. I have driven a 10,000 ton warship, stood a few feet from a jet taking off from an aircraft carrier and been underwater on a submarine. Day in and day out I am exceptionally proud to have had a chance to be part of, and represent, the U.S. Navy as it carries out its missions around the world. From my experience, I believe that if you want to do this job/career/position when you grow up, you need to realize your actions now will affect what you can do later. In testimony to a House Armed Service subcommittee in 2009, Dr. Curtis Gilroy, Director of Accession Policy, Office of the Undersecretary of Defense for Personnel and Readiness said that 75% of America's youth do not meet the requirements for the military. 18% are excluded specifically because of drug or alcohol problems. Medical situations (including obesity), criminal activity, low aptitude, and dependents who cannot be accommodated early in a career are also significant factors. Some of these things you can not affect, others you can. Drug use, criminal activity, and a lack of physical fitness can easily prevent you from joining the military, and are decisions you make.—Lt. Frederick Martin, U.S. Navy public affairs officer[24]

For my job/career, I provide medical care to patients, both when they are ill and when they are relatively healthy, by advising them how to maintain and/or improve their health. The attributes that are needed for me to succeed in this position include: the ability to process and remember large amounts of information; good listening skills and the ability to empathize with others' experiences in life; steady hands for performing examinations and surgical procedures; and the dedication to search for answers when they are not readily apparent. The best thing about this career is that I can save lives and help improve the quality of people's lives. From my experience, I believe that if you want to have this career when you grow up, you must embrace responsibility and practice healthy habits yourself, because people will one day see YOU as a role model . . . you don't want to disappoint them, OR YOURSELF.—Darya Alexander, MD, family physician[25]

After more than a decade in the world of international finance in which I amassed 2 master's degrees (including an MBA from Harvard) and countless frequent flyer miles, I decided to help raise 3 boys and try to keep our family life flowing smoothly. The attributes that are needed for me to succeed in this position include attention to detail, multitasking, a sense of humor, and belief that children are a gift from God. The best thing about this career/job/position is the importance of trying to shape tomorrow's minds. From my experience, I believe that if you want to do this job/career/position when you grow up, you need to realize that fulfillment comes in small increments throughout life. Anything that is worthwhile takes effort, time, and commitment.—Alex, CEO of three boys[26]

I worked for a ski mountain in Vail, Colorado. The attributes needed for this job were: being able to lift 50 pounds, being a clear thinker, being able to think on your feet, being a good skier (you have to take a ski test) and you must be able to work well with people, be friendly, responsible (if you don't show up twice you're fired) and you have to be able to handle outdoor weather.

The benefits? Free ski lift tickets, being outside, being around people.—John, ski lift manager[27]

For my job/career I have been involved in the apparel business selling a variety of products to the retail marketplace. The attributes that are needed for me to succeed in this position include persistence, people skills, and a knowledge of the markets that I am involved in. Developing trusting relationships with my customers and achieving the internal goals of my company are two key factors that I focus on to succeed. Also, the ability to deal with multiple, complex issues with creative solutions is required. The best thing about this career/job/position is that I get to work with great brands and retailers in a fast-paced environment in New York City. From my experience, I believe that if you want to do this job/career/position when you grow up you must have a passion for the wholesale/retail trade. In addition, you will need to manage a variety of personalities both internally and externally that require you to be sharp at all times. Focusing your energies on the task at hand requires a clear mind and a steady hand—something that becomes nearly impossible if you are under the influence of drugs or alcohol.—Jalil Keval, vice president of sales[28]

For my job/career I am a nature/portrait photographer, freelance writer, and raise three daughters at home. The attributes that are needed for me to succeed in this position include the ability to balance family commitments with creative drive, the ability to focus when the time is right, organizational skills, the ability to say no to things that aren't in my range of focus (never easy!), and unending patience and understanding. The best thing about this career/job/position is the opportunity to be giving to people I love almost constantly, the chance to express my creative side in ways that I enjoy . . . and also that other people seem to enjoy, as well, and with taking pictures/writing, the chance to be artistic in a flexible way—working early in the morning or late at night, and doing something that is extremely meaningful to me.

From my experience, I believe that if you want to do this job/career/position when you grow up, you should believe that a clear mind, strong focus, and huge commitment to your goals, along with a nurturing, loving, patient heart will take you very far in terms of feeling like your life's work has meaning.—Jennifer Bergen, mom/photographer/writer[29]

For my job/career I am a police officer. The attributes that are needed for me to succeed in this position include an understanding of people and ability to effectively communicate. The best thing about this career/job/position is making a difference to people in need of assistance in some way. From my experience, I believe that if you want to do this job/career/position when you grow up, you need to be compassionate and caring.—Tom Frank, police chief[30]

For my job/career I was a prosecutor for 25 years (charging children and adults with crimes). Presently I'm a judge. The attributes that are needed for me to succeed in this position include listening, making timely decisions, and being able to give reasons for my decisions. I also need to be very level—in the tone of my voice and my reactions to the litigants. The best thing about this career/job/position is sometimes I am part of making changes (positive ones) in a person's life and resolve problems for people fairly. From my experience, I believe that if you want to do this job/career/position when you grow up you have to work hard, show leadership qualities, live a law abiding life, know how to say no to friends who take risks that endanger their safety. Remember that a poor decision that can just take one second to make, can change your life forever as well as your family's and friend's.—Sandy Williams, Ozaukee County Circuit Court judge, Wisconsin[31]

For my job/career I manage the "business aspects" of a performing arts center. The center is a school district facility but it is also used extensively by several community organizations and hosts a visiting artist series of national/international touring artists. The attributes that are needed for me to succeed in this position include reliability, organization, creativity, a clear mind, excellent customer service, and communication skills, the ability to focus and pay very close attention to details. The best thing about this career/job/position is my job always provides new and exciting challenges. Every artist, organization, customer, coworker, patron, volunteer, vendor, student, performance, or event adds something to our "memory book." Being a performing arts center, the creativity and energy that is close at hand on a daily basis makes for a very exciting job. From my experience, I believe that if you want to do this job/career/position when you grow up, you need to remain focused and always have a very clear mind so that your creativity can blossom. The competition that exists in every aspect of life (job, school, athletics, etc.) is so great that you need to do everything possible to make yourself the best you can be.—Kathleen Koster, coordinator and box office manager[32]

For my job/career I write a newspaper column and books, and work for a "think tank," an organization that analyzes public policy issues. The attributes that are needed for me to succeed in this position include writing ability, logic, creativity, diligence, a sense of humor. The best thing about this career/job/position is I think it sometimes makes a difference, causes people to think about issues or other people or the world in a different way—at least occasionally. From my experience, I believe that if you want to do this job/career/position when you grow up, you need to stay focused, be flexible, have confidence in yourself and your abilities—all things that pretty much demand a clear, drug-free mind.—Mike Nichols, writer[33]

For my job/career I work for a large mutual insurance company. There I lead a team that researches, builds tools, and reports on compensation for our distribution system. The attributes that are needed for me to succeed in this position include self-motivated, analytical, hard worker, ability to direct work of team members and prioritize work. Be responsive to clients' needs and balance that with effort and resources. Also need the ability to translate technical ideas and solutions into language our clients can understand. The best thing about this career/job/position is I get to work with smart people that continue to challenge and motivate me to learn more and be a better person. I also get to lead a remarkable team! From my experience, I believe that if you want to do this job/career/position when you grow up, work hard and be self-motivated. You also have to seek opportunity and put yourself out there for it. Don't be afraid to raise your hand and volunteer. The world won't wait for you, jump in!—Jane, business consultant/manager[34]

For my job/career I am the owner and creative director for a marketing and branding firm working primarily for consumer products companies. The attributes that are needed for me to succeed in this position include hard work, leadership abilities, focused creativity, staying healthy, excellent presentation and communication skills. The best thing about this career/job/position is seeing my work at the grocery store, Walgreens or on a billboard and remembering the exact time I thought of the idea. Sometimes my best ideas come from driving my Thunderbird convertible. From my experience, I believe that if you want to do this job/career/position when you grow up you have to stay focused, work hard and go to college! You must volunteer and take an internship to start a network. Forming a business network is so important. Even though my job is highly creative, I am still a business person and work with executive-level business people. My clients expect me to be on the leading edge of social media and technology so that I can provide them with good creative ideas that enable them to grow their businesses. To do my job, you need to have boundless energy, think creatively within a business environment, and know a little bit about a lot of stuff!—Paula Hare, owner and creative director for Hare Strigenz Inc. and Paula Hare and Associates[35]

My job/career is law enforcement. The attributes that are needed for me to succeed in this position include PR skills and the ability to read non-verbal body language. Thick skin. Ability to work long/odd hours, holidays, weekends with little sleep. Function, without failure, during high stress situations. Mental and physical toughness. Compassion and perspective. The best thing about this career/job/position is for me it's a paycheck with diminishing benefits . . . no more, no less. From my experience, I believe that if you want to do this job/career/position when you grow up, you expose yourself to as many life experiences as possible. Sports, social settings, culturally diverse settings. Enhance leadership skills. Learn about human dysfunction . . . if you become a cop you will become an expert in it. Stay out of legal trouble. Pre-employment background checks will reveal all of the skeletons in the closet.—Sgt. Kip Butler, police sergeant[36]

For my job/career I help businesses transform themselves so they can better compete in the marketplace. The attributes that are needed for me to succeed in this position include a solid education, a great reputation, ability to learn quickly and adapt to new environments, and ability to work well with people. The best thing about this career/job/position is it never gets boring, and it pays me lots of money so I can provide for my family and so I can afford to buy the fun things in life, like a cool car and great vacations. From my experience, I believe that if you want to do this job/career/position when you grow up, you need to focus on your goal and realize that everything you do, from your teen years through your adult life, will either help or hurt your chances of reaching your goal. Live every day

Substance Abuse Reflections and Regrets

"The only thing I regret the most is ever being at that one party when I was 14 or 15 years old. I now think to myself if I had not been there at that point and time I would have not done the things I've done or I might not be where I'm at today. One lesson related to my experience that will help me in life is seeing how much of a better person I am without drugs and or alcohol. If I had known that drugs and alcohol were so addictive to the human race I would have not even messed around with the stuff to begin with."—Kyle[37]

"Biggest regret was hurting my family, and losing soccer."—Brady[38]

"Powerless, weak, broken beyond repair, my life is out of control, unmanageable, and finally dead to the world and to myself. If I had known something I didn't know before picking up using it would have been that: 'the drugs I'm about to pick up and put in my body will haunt me for the rest of my life. These drugs will do nothing but lie and hurt me and the ones I care around me. These drugs will end up almost costing my life and or will cost me my life, these drugs will end me up in jail/prison due to my obsession to you, these drugs will consume me whole and wither and decay me as a human being. If I shall die due to my use I would be just another sad statistic. These drugs will overpower my thoughts and every right decision to do well. I will lose all control in my life and my life will be totally unmanageable and miserable. These drugs will make me live every day like it should be my last and I shall live like I am dying because these drugs are digging myself an early grave.' Those are all the things I can think of that I wish I had had the insight in before I ever started using substances. I personally think teens need a firsthand view on what will happen if you continue down this path of self-destruction. A mentor or a recovering addict themselves should be their guide and help them understand substance abuse and share with them insights into their own experience using, to help them with their own demons. Teens need to know they are not alone and they do not have to jeopardize their selves to these awful things. That they have their whole life ahead of them and why ruin that freedom by being controlled by a never-ending substance addiction. That they should stop while they still can if they haven't gone too far already. They should seek help as soon as possible and listen to the rest of society and us recovering addicts. I know as once a stubborn teenager I hated and despised any and all authority figures but we should get over our selfishness and stubbornness against the world and listen if anything to what insight we have to give you. That is my best advice I can possibly give to anyone trying to recover from substance abuse."—Princess Peach[39]

"There was once a time that she was the first thing I thought of when I awoke, where every minute without her seemed like the clock was broke. The things she put me through one would only do for true love and when she'd kiss my consciousness it was like the touch of a peaceful dove. But when that bird would leave and fly away my love and kindness couldn't even make her stay and I'd long for maybe just one feather something to get me through the day; through the miserable and nasty weather. The hurt and longing; the racing thoughts and burning tears; the chewed off fingernails, curled toes couldn't ever take away the pain. I would try to let my blood flow only red but I just itched to slide that heaven filled needle through my vein. I had to cash a check, make an ATM withdrawal get the money to my hand and make the anxious call. Food was not important nor that I hadn't showered yet. I had to hold the syringe, so powerful. The transit so smooth hold the lighter under her under the dark and shiny spoon as soon as I smelled her cooling tasted the scent roll down my throat I started to feel better. It soothed me like a vibrating piano note. As I injected her she pulled down on my arms made them weigh a zillion pounds. Kicked me in the head just enough so that I wasn't dead. Her kiss is that of pleasure but when she pulls away one of pure misery. I loved her for a while thought I'd never leave her side. But I too pulled away and now she wished I would have died. She haunts me every night always visible like a lighthouse light."—creative writing by Angela[40]

with honor, stay far away from illegal substances or anything where you have even the slightest chance of doing something you would someday regret, and lastly, build your rock-solid reputation one day at a time.—WS, management consultant[41]

For my job/career I teach reading to kids who struggle. I love it because I can see progress and growth in my students, every day. The attributes that are needed for me to succeed in this position include flexibility, responsibility, and self-efficacy. It also helps to be well-organized in the teaching profession. The best thing about this career/job/position is knowing that I am making a difference in children's lives. Also, historically, a career in education provides job security and great health insurance. Although these things might not seem important when you are in your teens, they are incredibly important things to consider when looking into your future. From my experience, I believe that if you want to do this job/career/position when you grow up, you need to stay in school, work hard, and stay true to yourself. Good grades are important, but they aren't everything.

> "Myth: It only happens to people who have a criminal disposition."—Tom Frank, chief of police

Learn more about yourself and the great possibilities that lie ahead for you and within you.

Always remember that there are multiple intelligences in this world. Some people are book smart, some are art smart, people smart, musically smart, mechanically smart . . . the list goes on and on. Believe in yourself and in YOUR intelligence. You will go far.—Helen Butler, reading intervention specialist[42]

Closing This Chapter

How do you feel after reading all of this? What do you think? How have your thoughts and feelings come together to create a possible new perspective? Lots of people have shared lots of thoughts about this issue . . . for you. Hopefully, as you take it all in, you continue to inquire and are inspired to learn more about yourself and the great possibilities that lie ahead for you and within you.

> "I offer you peace. I offer you love. I offer you friendship. I see your beauty. I hear your need. I feel your feelings. My wisdom flows from the Highest Source. I salute that Source in you. Let us work together for unity and love."—Mahatma Gandhi, leader (India) for nonviolence

Notes

1. Whitnie Bestor was in high school at the time of her written contribution, 2013.
2. Kaiti Bestor was in high school at the time of her written contribution, 2013.
3. Hailie Bestor was in fifth grade at the time of her written contribution, 2013.
4. Kyle was out of high school at the time of his written contribution, 2012.
5. Brady was out of high school at the time of his written contribution, 2012.
6. Jessica was out of high school at the time of her phone interview, 2012.
7. Kyle was out of high school at the time of his interview and written contribution, 2012.
8. Princess Peach was out of high school at the time of her interview and written contribution, 2012.
9. Pandit Rajmani Tigunait, PhD, spiritual head, Himalayan Institute, contributed in February 2013.
10. Janet Osherow, LICSW, family services coordinator, provided her written contribution and phone interview in 2012.
11. John Mabry, SAC-IT, provided his written contribution and phone interview in 2012.
12. Bonnie shared during an interview in 2012.
13. Tom Frank shared his thoughts in an interview in 2012.
14. Alisa shared her thoughts in an interview in 2012.
15. Ryan Byrne, MD, shared his written contribution in 2012.

16. Reverend Kenneth Wheeler provided his written contribution in 2012.
17. Dr. Gabor Maté, MD, provided his written contribution in 2012.
18. Tim contributed through a phone interview in 2012.
19. Kyle provided his written contribution in 2012.
20. Karen Glassman, MSW, MB, shared her written contribution in 2012.
21. Brady contributed to the book in 2012.
22. Steve Heston provided his written contribution in 2012.
23. Paul provided his written contribution in 2012.
24. Frederick Martin provided his written contribution in 2012.
25. Darya Alexander, MD, provided her written contribution in 2012.
26. Alex provided her written contribution in 2012.
27. John provided his written contribution in 2012.
28. Jalil Keval provided his written contribution in 2012.
29. Jennifer Bergen provided her written contribution in 2012.
30. Tom Frank provided his written contribution in 2012.
31. Sandy Williams provided her written contribution in 2012.
32. Kathleen Koster provided her written contribution in 2012.
33. Mike Nichols provided his written contribution in 2012.
34. Jane provided her written contribution in 2012.
35. Paula Hare provided her written contribution in 2012.
36. Kip Butler provided his written contribution in 2012.
37. Kyle provided his written contribution in 2012.
38. Brady provided his written contribution in 2012.
39. Princess Peach provided her contribution in 2012.
40. Angela's mother Bonnie provided Angela's written contribution in 2012.
41. WS provided his written contribution in 2012.
42. Helen Butler provided her written contribution in 2012.

FROM THE PERSPECTIVE OF . . .

....

"A wise man's question contains half the answer."
—*Solomon Ibn Gabirol Ben, philosopher*

In this chapter you'll read words from "a dad" and "a mom." From "a sister," a "pastor," and "a police officer." You'll hear from "a brother." You'll learn how these people feel toward the person or people in their lives who was/were dealing with substance abuse issues. Perhaps you will see a common theme here. About human fragility. About love. About reaching out. About letting someone in.

From the Perspective of . . .

A Dad

"When I was a boy of fourteen, my father was so ignorant I could hardly stand to have the old man around. But when I got to be twenty-one, I was astonished at how much the old man had learned in seven years."—*Mark Twain*

This is one of my favorite quotes. I found it to apply to my own father, and I hope as my daughters get older they will witness me "learning" much. Part of being a teenager and becoming a young adult is to start formulating your own opinions and making your own decisions. Decisions on everything from what to wear to school to more consequential decisions as who you are friends with and what your plans are for your future. And as this book addresses, decisions about drugs and alcohol. If you are fortunate, as you start this process, you will have a father, mother, uncle, aunt, older sibling, or teacher, who will be there, whether you ask for it or not, trying to influence your decisions. I'm sure you have experienced

"It's about reaching out, and letting someone in . . . "

this already. And I'm also sure you have agreed with some of the guidance you have received, but just as often, and maybe more, you have thought us adults don't understand your life or what it is like to be a teen today. And our advice is not relevant, wise, or useful to you. As a father, and on behalf of the adults in your life, I plead with you not to dismiss our guidance. We are only motivated by seeing you happy and peaceful. Our views and ultimately our advice concerning drugs and alcohol have been formed through personal mistakes or regrets, or from living through friends and family members suffering physically, mentally and even death from the effects of drugs and alcohol. When you find yourself dismissing our advice, realize we may know or have experienced something you haven't yet. And although we may seem out of touch or even foolish, be patient with us for a few years. You will find we are astonishingly fast learners.—Scott Bestor[1]

A Mom

Where did you go? One day you were a boy collecting frogs, doing puzzles, and forgetting to clear your dishes. You also were the adventurous one, the one that took off down the drainage tube that headed who knows where but definitely underground. I can still hear your brothers and sisters yell-ing at you to come back. There is also the memory of me, smiling at a certain level at your adventurous spirit. I liked it. I liked that you took risks and tried things and were not afraid of life. It was a quality that I felt had been squished in me and I certainly didn't want to squish it in you. Naturally I wanted you to be smart about your risks and I remember really thinking a lot about how to help you be smart about them without creating a fear-filled crouching boy. I truly loved watching you. I figured that you could probably teach me what I needed to know about you. And you did.

I turned my head for a moment and you became a man/boy. I was pretty sure you were the same person, the same spirit, the same soul, the same exploring, expanding, maturing boy—and something was way different.

You stopped talking to me, you stopped showing me things, you stopped being happy, you stopped teaching me and you started grunting at me when I talked to you. Oh how I missed you. I missed the curious, creative and caring you. I missed the happy you.

Unbeknownst to you, I didn't have a clue what to do. I noticed, I watched, I tried to engage you and for the most part I received that uninterested grunt. This much I knew . . . I honestly, really, couldn't believe it, didn't have any control. I couldn't figure out how to protect you from all the "bad" decisions you could make—without squishing you down into a prescribed way of being in the world. Quite truthfully, I had to decide if I was going to guilt you, shame you or otherwise manipulate you into doing what I wanted you to do. Or was I going to watch, listen, and allow nature to take its course—allow natural consequences to be the teacher, the "bad guy." I really wanted to be able to control all of it. But why?

Well there was this thing about being a parent that culture defines. The culture says that if your kid is getting in trouble, doing drugs, drinking alcohol—then you are a bad parent. And if you are a bad parent, then that most likely renders you a bad person. The culture says that it is the fault of the parent.

It was a very interesting time inside me. I knew that I had given everything I had to create something unique and special for my family. I knew that it was far from perfect however, it was mindful, thoughtful, non-reactive—life giving, not life taking parenting. Something inside me said that it really had been good enough.

Then I asked myself—well, what!!!! What is going on then? What!!!! I screamed to myself. I just couldn't see it, at least at first. Then gradually I realized that this really had nothing to do with me being good enough or even not good enough. It had to do with your choice to get involved in drugs. I needed to remind myself that this was not a reflection of who I was, but was a reflection of who you were. And you were still the creative, adventurous, and spirited boy that I had had the privilege to watch up until then.

With this realization finally in place, I was able to return to being a parent to you. A parent with all her perfect imperfections again watching, listening and waiting. So I used the best I had to decide when to get involved and when to let the nature of reality kick in. I really really wanted you to find your way with as few obstacles as possible.

Not the case though. And this was not something I could control anyway, for some reason, you needed to move through your teens the hard way. I was immeasurably sad, I was terrified and sometimes I was consumed by anger. I learned that those were my feelings and that the feelings were my own response to actions that you were taking.

And that I was responsible for my feelings—not you.

My observation was that you seemed to want to escape, hide and otherwise buck the system. Truth be told—you were only bucking yourself.

I guess you just didn't believe me when I warned you. I warned you that there was a strong family addiction pattern from my side of the family. I told you how my sister died and my mother died. I can only guess that you must have thought that you could control it and have some fun.

I am desperately relieved that you are not in prison. I am desperately relieved that you are not indentured to a court system that will do whatever it needs to do to swallow you up and spit you out.

As your parent, everything inside me wanted to protect you from as many of the harsh realities of life. If I am completely honest—I wanted to protect myself from how horrible I would feel if I lost you. That is such a weird one. Your life and how you experience it is solely yours. I knew I needed to get out of the way.

There is no way you can possibly understand what it is like to be on my side of this fence. It's hard. It's particularly hard once you climbed over the fence and we seemed on opposite sides. As an adult that is supposed to be the responsible one, I finally was facing all my sorting out of what I was actually responsible for and what I wasn't. For me, there was a fine line between being responsible and handing over self-responsibility to you. I mean, you really can't learn about it without doing it and you can't do it if I don't hand it over. My idea was to do it in increments. It seemed like your idea was to take it all at once.

That would be fine—if I could have figured out how to keep you safe through the transition.

So far I wasn't seeing adult material in you. I was seeing avoiding, running away, escaping, avoiding, not wanting to take care of yourself, avoiding. Did I say avoiding?

There are a lot of adults out there who never learned how to face their feelings, destructive thoughts, habitual reactions, or even their own wisdom speaking loud and clear. For me, this was no longer about controlling what you were doing; now it was about using your choices to teach you about life. Oh, I know, you thought you knew everything. You knew how hopeless it all was, you knew that nothing really mattered, you knew that life wasn't all it was cracked up to be and that it looked like a whole lot of work. And in a way you were right. From your perspective those beliefs all appeared absolutely true. Since you were so sure that there really wasn't much worth in all this crazy game and it appeared that you would just as soon toss it all out the window. The problem was that your perspective just wasn't the only perspective. I suppose that underneath it all that was the only real problem.

It's all so crazy, really. We're born, we're totally free. Yeah, we're totally dependent physically, but we're totally free emotionally, mentally, even spiritually. We scream when we are uncomfortable, we smile when we are pleased, we sleep when we're tired, and eat when we're hungry. We have no beliefs about life and the nature of things. We don't know anything—except pure seeing of what is. Then we grow more independent physically and more limited emotionally, mentally and spiritually too. We learn to control our emotions, sometimes attaching beliefs to them that they are bad. We learn that there are all kinds of facts—everywhere. Many of them conflictual—and I suppose, all of them made up. We learn that we are actually quite powerless, when in actuality we are more powerful than we can imagine. We learn that imagining is make believe and that make believe isn't real—when it is actually as real as we want to make it.

I wish I could have had this conversation with you. Some of this was developing in me, I just didn't understand, yet.

I could see that you believed a whole lot of stuff that just wasn't true. And I knew that you needed to figure it out yourself. How do I get out of the way and still accept you, accept the way, learn and trust that your lessons are within what actually happens? Ok, really hard. Really hard to let life unfold, to own my own experiences, feelings and perspectives and let you have yours. It appeared that you were getting away with it. It appeared that the rules apply to everyone else. It appeared that there was no big deal.

Unless, you messed up.

I remember a time when you were 15 years old and asked if two friends could sleep over. I had no problem with it and said sure. I don't really know how it came about, I actually wasn't interested in that. I was interested in the fact that you put me and the rest of your family at a huge risk with your risk taking.

Something woke me in the middle of the night, and something told me to check on the three of you. None of you were in the house. And my van wasn't in the garage. Not good. Your risk taking was now compromising the safety of the family. Not good. I figured that eventually you'd return and I knew that I'd be waiting. When you came driving up the street it was obvious that I had discovered your adventuring as I was standing in the lit window with arms crossed. Probably a clear sign that you had crossed the line. I rolled my eyes when you obviously slowed and then made the decision to drive right on past the driveway. I could only imagine the conversation between the three of you as you tried to figure out what to do next.

About 10 minutes later, you pulled into the driveway and I walked out to the van. Opening the passenger door I told your friends to get out of my van and to phone their dads to pick them up. I remember one of the boys saying something about not being able to call his dad in the middle of the night. I remember saying, call him or I'll call the police. You are not welcome in this house. The calls were made and they waited on the porch to be picked up.

Do you remember how I sent you to bed without saying anything? Do you remember that I woke you at 7:45am and told you to get dressed? Do you remember that we got in the car and I didn't say where we were going until you asked? You didn't know that I'd been sitting on the floor in the doorway to your room waiting until 7:45 to wake you. I was not going to take the risk that you would jeopardize the safety of your family again. And to social services we drove.

Then it's a big deal. Unless that is, you don't think that going to jail isn't a big deal. You definitely do not need to be responsible there. Far as I know you are told pretty much when you can do about almost anything. And maybe, you won't mess up that bad. When your friend injured someone while driving high, those people didn't care one single bit about your friend's future—they just wanted him to pay, big time, with his time.

And he did time, a stunning amount of time. So instead of going to college, dating, exploring his likes and dislikes—he hung out in a prison for 6 years, with someone with a uniform telling him when he would eat, sleep, take a shit—no privacy, no maturing, no life lessons teaching him what works and what doesn't.

My sense is that you didn't care. You only wanted to fit in. I guess that means that you cared more about feeling good and being accepted than about yourself. Do you know what I mean by that? I mean, keeping alive and well the parts of ourselves that create, treasuring the gifts that we have. Remembering that we have something to offer this crazy world, remembering that that something is extraordinary. My soul's need for expression, for peace, for joy is unlimited. I don't think I am unique in that. I know now that you wanted to be accepted. I acknowledge that I truly didn't know how to teach you self-acceptance because I still hadn't found a way to accept myself. I understand now that what was most important was that you felt accepted. It is an interesting aspect of teen culture—this acceptance thing. The culture seems to be very judgmental. Why are you all so hard on each other? You know we are all in this together. Everyone does better by offering a hand. You will too. Find authentic friends. Friends that accept you as you are. I knew that I had not given you all the tools you needed. I still didn't know what they all were. I also thought that you were absolutely capable of figuring out some of the steps. I believed that you were able and willing to find good people, authentic people to hang out with.

I suppose that if you are/were willing to sell your soul for a quick trip there wasn't anything really that I can do about it. Believe it or not, you are here for a reason. And it is a unique reason—one for you to discover. This planet needs your gifts, your unique flavor of expression, your desires to be manifested.

As you grew and experimented and avoided—I did too. Well not the avoiding part, as best I could. I kept paying attention, kept experimenting with how to honestly reach you and still honor you and your journey. I kept the communication open and let you know that you were very important to me.

Here's the beginning. After you had moved out and you were about 20 years old I looked at you one day and told you that I could tell that you were using. I told you how scared I was and how I knew that it wasn't up to me what you did. You were refreshingly honest with me! I felt a tinge of hope. Sitting on the front stoop of the house, we talked. I felt that I could really sense you again. It had been such a long time. If I remember correctly there were probably a few tears of relief. You assured me that you had everything under control and secretly I had my doubts. We hugged each other and said good-bye. Leaning into your car I said that I was here for you, I was willing to do whatever I could to help—and you needed to let me know when you were ready.

A few weeks later I was just doing my thing, probably studying as I was in school at that time, all of a sudden I knew I was supposed to call you and tell you that it was time to clean it up. I was actually surprised by the revelation. It had been pretty clear to me for years that I was to stay out of the way and wait for you to be ready. I picked up the phone and called and there was no answer. I was again surprised because the inner message was pretty strong and now you weren't even home. I went to bed.

The next morning I woke up dreaming. I dreamed of me saying exactly what I was going to say to you the night before. Word for word. It was so vivid and so clear I couldn't dismiss it. So I headed for the phone again.

You answered groggy. You didn't say much and I did my part. I told you what I needed to say. We hung up.

A couple of hours later I opened the front door to get some air. Surprised, I found you sitting there. You were dull, exhausted, and looked like hell. You just looked at me and I looked back. You nodded when I asked if you wanted to come in and we sat on the living room floor while you told me that your girlfriend had kicked you out of the apartment. When you told her that I knew you were using she became extremely upset. The plan was to do it yourselves. She had a whole plan of how you two would detox and how everything would be okay. I guess somewhere deep inside of you there was a knowing that you probably needed more help or support and that this plan was probably not too realistic about it all.

All I knew to do was repeat what I'd said on the phone. I told you that I would be willing to resolve your financial crisis (due to drug use) if you were willing to go to the local hospital and get detoxed, do 90 AA meetings in 90 days and work for me until you had repaid me everything.

I was surprised by my response when you said that you didn't think you had a choice. I absolutely believed that you did indeed have a choice and that there was no choice about it if you didn't acknowledge the other options. I said, "Well you do have a choice, you can keep doing what you are doing, you can try to do it on your own, you can . . ." and I trailed off. I said, "There are lots and lots of options here and maybe you need to take some time and consider them. It isn't my job to figure out all your options, that is yours." I sent you back to lay down and told you to let me know what you wanted. It didn't take but 10 minutes and you were in front of me.

Everything inside me wanted to just take control, to start to make decisions for you, all so that I could feel like everything was okay. I just wanted everything to be okay, I wanted you to be okay and I wanted your brothers and sisters to not come to me worried about you, I wanted this whole nightmare to go away. Truth was, it wasn't so much about what I wanted—it was about what you wanted.

When you told me you were ready, ready to go to the hospital, ready to do whatever you needed to do so that you could indeed live a life that would be the life you chose, not the life that just happens because you don't care. You wanted to be able to live life full on.

How happy can a person be? What measure of happiness can any of us hold? I found out that I am capable of feeling immense joy and happiness. And that joy and happiness is in direct proportion to the amount of sadness and grief that I had also felt for those 5 years.

Now, I am content. I know that you had a couple of relapses—you told me. You seemed ashamed, but I wasn't ashamed—I was amazed, amazed at your honesty, integrity, and how you consistently attended to your own joy. I see you living life on your own terms, and I see you creating, loving, and having fun. I see you telling jokes to your 5-year-old niece, I see you in a loving relationship, I see you and I am so happy you are in my life.

Don't believe everything you think. The trail of stories that we as human beings can create is not something to create a life from. Just watch what you think about, how you think about yourself, what you tell yourself. Change your mind. It's simple, and not necessarily easy. Look at all the energy you are putting into managing your life right now. Let go, imagine, create. We are all waiting for your own unique flavor and gifts. How much goodness can you have in your life? As much as you can imagine.

P.S. My son, he chose detox, 90 meetings in 90 days. He relapsed 2 times and turned it around right away. He attended meetings gradually decreasing the frequency for about 10 years. He was 20 years old when he showed up at my door asking for help. He took responsibility for his actions and accepted help. And, he is happy, creative, and clear—doing what he loves.—Jori Azinger, L.Ac.[2]

A Brother

I could see what was going on with my sisters, and I couldn't figure out why my parents ignored it. I don't think they knew what to do. I don't think everyone is capable of fixing things. They just gave and hoped. You look at your sister, and you wonder, "How can you take money from our parents and lie to them?" My reaction was to act out. Show my anger to my parents about what my sisters were doing. It was kind of like fast food, right then there was an issue, but 12 hours later it seemed like it was forgotten. Tomorrow it was a different issue. But 12 hours later, my sisters still had the problem.

I'm this kid and I'm watching the news and right on the news I see that my sister's boyfriend was shot by the police and so I start to wonder how is my sister and where is she. I just couldn't believe it.

I was worried if she was alive or dead. Then the cops call and I find out my sister has been picked up for prostitution. I learn that people will do anything for drugs. I felt disbelief, but I wasn't supposed to know this about my sister so I couldn't talk to anyone about it. Not even with my best friend.

What would I say to my sister? Back then, when I was just a kid and they were teens, I wouldn't say anything to my sister. Or, I would have said, "You are pathetic." That was the problem. I was angry and I didn't know what to do. I had no way to put everything that was going on into perspective.

If I could tell her something now, having the wisdom I have now versus then . . . I would tell her, "You have an addiction." And I would ask her to do stuff together but I'd say we would do it without using. I would be strong enough. And I would say, that "I realize, it wasn't your fault. I love you."—Tim[3]

A Pastor

I remain hopeful for humanity as a major paradigm shift is taking place. The youth I work with are already decades ahead of their parents' generation on acceptance of others and rejection of the "isms" that have historically held us back from whole (healthy) living. Compassion, open acceptance, respect, communication without judgment and fear, getting "high" on life. Engaging on a truly equal basis rather than authoritative control. Being honest about our own insecurities and doubts. Removing categories of age, religion, status, and embracing youth with unconditional acceptance and love. No barriers.—Pastor Janis Kinens[4]

A Police Sergeant

Working in law enforcement for 26 years I have personally witnessed the tragedies that occur because of drug use and abuse especially those involving teenagers. I have seen young, highly intelligent students start using drugs and then fail out of school and see their lives spiral out of control. I have also personally seen young kids I know die of overdoses. As a human being, how could I just stand by and let this epidemic continue to ruin lives without trying to stop it. Unfortunately sometimes treatment doesn't work, no matter how hard or how much money parents spend. Sometimes when treatment doesn't change the behavior the only thing that works is law enforcement arresting the teen and getting them into criminal justice system where they may end up in jail away from the drugs or in court ordered treatment with the fear of prison if they are not successful.

I am most often disappointed in them (teens) for making poor decisions. I can't really be angry, I usually save that anger for the dealers that target our young and impressionable kids to sell to solely for the purpose of making money, without even a thought of the lives they are ruining.

A couple years ago I was advised by our dispatcher that there was a gentleman in our lobby wishing to speak to me. I went out into our lobby and there stood a well-dressed man and he asked if I remembered him. I apologized and said that I didn't, and he then told me his name. I immediately recognized his name as someone who I had dealt with many years ago when he was 15 and had taken him into custody for selling drugs to friends. I remembered that he had also been using drugs pretty heavily and was now selling drugs to pay for his own drugs to use. I told him he looked good and asked what he was doing now. He went on to explain that he was in town visiting family and wanted to stop and thank me for stopping him when I did. He said that I easily could have pushed for him to be criminally charged, but instead he went into treatment. He said his mom moved him out of state to his grandparents' home where he could get away from the group of friends he was hanging around with. He said he went into treatment and ended up graduating from high school with honors. He went on to college and then medical school and he handed me his business card, and he is now a heart surgeon.

At that moment I knew that every bad day I have had at work over the years was worth it. It is also important for kids who are using to know they may feel like their lives are spinning out of control but need to realize that there is a way out. That young man is the perfect example. Drug addiction does not have to be a life sentence. With proper counseling help, support and life changes, they too can turn their lives around and become successful adults. This is not the only success story I have seen over the years. I now talk to former users who have gotten help and are now healthy adults with spouses, children, and careers. All it takes is for the teen to want to change, they have to make that decision for the resources available to be effective.—Rick Leach, police sergeant, southeastern Wisconsin[5]

A Sister

Hello,

I am Patricia Bittner, the Methamphetamine Community Policing Coordinator, for the Leech Lake Tribal Police Department on the Leech Lake Reservation.

In this position I go into the schools and communities to educate the young and old about the harmful effects that Methamphetamine use has on people. I have been doing this for the past year now and because I have educated our young people about meth I wanted to come up with a slogan that was catchy and on the lighter side. So I came up with, "Don't Meth with Me, I'm Drug Free!"

10% of the people who try alcohol for the FIRST time will become addicted.

98% of the people who try Methamphetamines for the FIRST time will become addicted.

This highly addictive drug will have you; sprung, thirsty, fiending, spun, all doped, and snaked, after you tried just ONCE!

When you live the drug life you will be beaten, raped, shot, stabbed, go to jail/prison, and death will slowly sneak up on you. I know this because my baby sister and her husband had all the monkeys on their backs. The pipes/needles were calling their names, and the devil was knocking at their door.

In October 2006 the devil succeeded and took them away from us. We buried my baby sister in the cemetery by my house. Every day that I drive

Don't meth with me!

by her grave makes me want to fight the war on drugs a lot harder than the day before.

My message to all the young people in this world is: you will be our future leaders running this country, we are counting on you, so make us proud and, "Don't Meth around with drugs!"

Don't ever forget you are loved and wanted by many!

Sincerely,

Patricia Bittner[6]

Closing This Chapter

Perhaps reading these thoughts from these folks helps you to see how others may feel about substance abuse issues. Maybe you were surprised by how they felt. If you, or someone you love, is dealing with such issues, those around and in your life may be supportive, understanding, and people to turn to.

Notes

1. Scott Bestor shared his written contribution in 2012.
2. Jori Azinger shared her written contribution in 2012.
3. Tim shared his written contribution in 2012.
4. Pastor Janis Kinens shared his written contribution in 2012.
5. Rick Leach shared his written contribution in 2012.
6. Patricia Bittner shared her written contribution in 2013.

The End

"Whoever you are, there is some younger person who thinks you are perfect. There is some work that will never be done if you don't do it. There is someone who would miss you if you were gone. There is a place that you alone can fill."—Jacob M. Braude, author

When I first began writing this book, I had no idea where it would lead. I did not know how I would find people who would contribute to the book in ways that I knew would make the book the most truthful. After all, when this book was being written, addiction and the problems associated with it were still judged to some degree, and so I wondered if anyone would come forth and offer to help, share his thoughts, and even her experiences for a book such as this.

The first person I approached to contribute was a friend and past coworker who holds a position in law enforcement and who is highly respected in the town in which I live. His receptivity was immediate. He shared his own insights and then gave me names of others who he believed would help too. Those names led to more people who were open and willing to help. People who are experts on one side of the war on drugs, and then the teens who were brave enough and generous enough to share that they were seemingly on the other side because they were the addicted.

The final person who shared his words is a teacher who has lectured and taught worldwide, is an author, and one from whom I have learned and continue to learn *life*. He is honored and respected around the globe. He sent his words from India:

As a teacher, I remind you that you are a wonderful person. You have the potential to become anything you wish. Once you realize the innate wisdom of your body and immense power of your mind, you can accomplish anything. Once you discover the joy your soul embodies, you will not be dependent on any substance in the world. I also remind you that substance abuse is not a sin. In fact, it is not even an abuse of a substance, per se. It is the abuse of your body and the abuse of your mind. Your body and mind are a gift from God. Celebrate life as it was given to you, and aspire to achieve more. And you can do that without using any foreign substance as a crutch. The power that is within you can drive away all of your fears

Only in your seeking will you continue to find the way. You always have, and always will, hold the key.

and doubts. Once you discover the Divinity in you, you will never suffer from loneliness. You have the power to design your destiny. You *can* do it, and therefore, my friends, do it! May God bless you with the power and intelligence and the brilliance that is in you, and that is you."[1]—Pandit Rajmani Tigunait, PhD, spiritual head, Himalayan Institute

Through these words and all of those shared in this book by the ever-expanding network of people from around the world that came forth, I began to realize that there is hope within what is referred to as a war on drugs. The peace is that all of these people are striving for the same thing and the hope is that together it can be achieved. Perhaps we no longer call it a "war" because at the end of the day, we are all ultimately working together for the eradication of this disease.

Remember at the beginning of the book when you read about finding out what happened to the "good guys"? Well, you found out a lot about all the good people in this book, the adults who shared their feelings, the teens who were addicted. Everyone, they're all "the good guys."

Therefore, there really aren't sides. Everyone is in this together working toward a common goal. Perhaps realizing this is the first step toward healing, on so many levels.

So, what happened to you through the process of reading this book? Did anything shift for you? Do you feel you have more answers, and therefore, more questions? Did you learn more about yourself?

If this book helped open your eyes to different ways of thinking and helped those with experiences be able to share with others, then it has served its purpose. If it helped answer some questions, then it served its purpose as well. I hope that beyond this, it has inspired you to ask more questions. Because I've come to realize that only in your seeking will you continue to find the way. You always have, and always will, hold the key.

Best on your journey.

Live Your Light.[2]

Sheri.

Notes

1. Pandit Rajmani Tigunait, PhD, spiritual head of Himalayan Institute, shared in a written contribution sent from India in February 2013, during the Kumbha Mela.
2. Balancing Arts Studio, Sheri Mabry Bestor, Registered Mark.

Appendix A:
More Facts at a Glance

Teens, here is a chance to read some more eye-opening facts on substances from the National Institute on Drug Abuse that might make you stop and think.

Alcohol

As you know, alcohol can affect your brain and your body. It is absorbed into your bloodstream and reaches vital organs, which it can damage. It can lead to loss of coordination, slowed reflexes, poor vision, losing your memory, and blacking out. Because it depresses your central nervous system, it impairs your judgment, so you may not have the ability to avoid risky behavior. If you drink too much at one time, or if you drink alcohol too fast, you can get alcohol poisoning, which can put you in a coma or kill you. Alcohol mixed with other drugs is also really dangerous—even something you wouldn't necessarily think of, like acetaminophen, which is found in fever and pain medicine, can cause problems when combined with alcohol. This is just the beginning of the dangers of alcohol.

In addition to what it can do negatively to your body and brain, don't forget that drinking under age is illegal. You can fail a breath test with one drink, and can lose your driver's license, have to pay a fine, get kicked off sports at school, be suspended, and have to take community classes.

Why is drinking under a certain age illegal? Drinking under age is illegal for good reason, because teens' brains aren't finished growing. Neither are their bodies. People who begin drinking at an earlier age are more likely to have drinking problems later on in life. Other names: juice, hooch, hard stuff, brewskis, brews, sauce, booze.

Source: NIDA, "Drugs, Brains, and Behavior: The Science of Addiction," www.drugabuse.gov/publications/science-addiction/addiction-health (accessed 2012).

Anabolic Steroids

Buying "bulk" is never a good deal when it comes to these substances, which can cause guys to grow breasts and girls to grow beards along with more life-threatening effects.

Ever wondered how those bulky weight lifters got so big? While some may have gotten their muscles through a strict regimen of weight lifting and diet, others may have gotten that way through the illegal use of anabolic-androgenic steroids. *Anabolic* refers to steroids' ability to help build muscle, and *androgenic* refers to their role in promoting the development of male sexual characteristics. Other types of steroids, like cortisol, estrogen, and progesterone, do not build muscle, are not anabolic, and therefore do not have the same harmful effects.

Anabolic-androgenic steroids are usually synthetic substances similar to the male sex hormone testosterone. They do have legitimate medical uses. Sometimes doctors prescribe them to help people with certain kinds of anemia and men who don't produce enough testosterone on their own. But doctors never prescribe anabolic steroids to young, healthy people to help them build muscles. Without a prescription from a doctor, anabolic steroids are illegal. Street names for steroids are "roids" and "juice."

Source: NIDA, "Facts on Drugs: Anabolic Steroids," http://teens.drugabuse.gov/drug-facts/anabolic-steroids.

Brain and Addiction

Discover what's in your head and how drugs of abuse cause changes in the brain.

All drugs of abuse—nicotine, cocaine, marijuana, and others—affect the brain's "reward" circuit, which is part of the limbic system. Normally, the reward circuit responds to pleasurable experiences by releasing the neurotransmitter dopamine, which creates feelings of pleasure and tells the brain that this is something important—pay attention and remember it. Drugs hijack this system, causing unusually large amounts of dopamine to flood the system. Sometimes, this lasts for a long time compared to what happens when a natural reward stimulates dopamine. This flood of dopamine is what causes the "high" or euphoria associated with drug abuse.

Club Drugs

Have you heard of raves? Raves are all-night dance parties, concerts, or night clubs where people gather and a wide array of drugs are used. Club drugs have all differing affects, including amnesia. (GHB and Rohypnol are used in date rape.

Date rape is when someone puts something into your drink or otherwise gets you to ingest a drug, and then is able to take advantage of you sexually, without your coherent consent.) Club drugs can affect your brain and body, causing damage and even death. Club drugs are produced in a way that makes it challenging to know what chemicals are used, and therefore, the dangers are unknown. Higher doses of club drugs can kill you. Other names: Rohypnol—Roofies, R-2. Katmine—K, Special K, Ket, Vitamin K, Kit Kat. Ecstasy—Ex, X, XTC. GHB—Liquid Ecstasy, Liquid X, Grievous Bodily Harm, Georgia Home Boy.

Source: NIDA, "Drugs, Brains, and Behavior: The Science of Addiction," www.drugabuse.gov/publications/science-addiction/addiction-health (accessed 2012).

Cocaine

Using cocaine can give you a quick high but then a deep low, with strong feelings of depression. It can make you feel angry or anxious, keep you from sleeping, and make you not eat regularly. Because cocaine involves the part of the brain that processes chemicals that make you enjoy and feel pleasure, you begin to have an increased need for the drug to attain the same effect. Some of the physical effects also include strokes, heart attacks, and death. Other names: toot, snow, rock (crack), lines, powder, coke, dust, blow.

Source: NIDA, "Drugs, Brains, and Behavior: The Science of Addiction," www.drugabuse.gov/publications/science-addiction/addiction-health (accessed 2012).

Ecstasy (MDMA)

This club drug can cause confusion, depression, sleep problems, intense fear, and anxiety that can last for days or weeks (in regular drug users) after taking it.

"Ecstasy" is a slang term for MDMA, short for 3,4-methylenedioxymethamphetamine, a name that's nearly as long as the all-night parties where MDMA is often used. That's why MDMA has been called a "club drug." It has effects similar to those of other stimulants, and it often makes the person feel like everyone is his or her friend, even when that's not the case.

HIV, AIDS, and Drug Abuse

HIV is a blood-borne virus. That means it can spread when the blood or bodily fluids of someone who's infected comes in contact with the blood, broken skin, or mucous membranes of an uninfected person. Sharing needles or other equipment used for injection drug use and engaging in risky sexual behaviors are the two main ways that HIV is spread.

Source: NIDA for Teens, "Facts on Drugs, HIV, Aids, and Drug Abuse," http://teens.drugabuse.gov/drug-facts/hiv-aids-and-drug-abuse.

Hallucinogens

Hallucinogens have an effect on how your brain functions and how you take in information. They affect the way your body moves, the way you develop and grow, the way hormones are produced. They affect the way you perceive information coming in. Your brain may imagine things that don't exist such as voices talking or images. Hallucinogens can cause affects that can occur years later. The use of these drugs increases your heart rate and raises your blood pressure, and can affect your heart and lung by causing failure. You can go into a coma. You can die. Other names: Lysergic Acid Diethylamide—LSD, blotter, acid. Ecstasy—E, X, XTC. Phencyclidine—PCP, angel dust, boat, ozone. Psilocybin—magic mushrooms, shrooms.

Source: NIDA, "Drugs, Brains, and Behavior: The Science of Addiction," www.drugabuse.gov/publications/science-addiction/addiction-health (accessed 2012).

Heroin

Heroin slows; it slows everything from your reaction time to your overall thinking as well as your memory. Heroin enters the brain quickly, and any way you take it, be it injecting, smoking, swallowing, or snorting, can lead to a quick addiction. Heroin kills, and some studies say that it ranks as one of the top two reported drugs found in deaths from drug abuse. Other names: black tar, big h, dope, skag, mud, brown sugar, horse, smack.

Source: NIDA, "Drugs, Brains, and Behavior: The Science of Addiction," www.drugabuse.gov/publications/science-addiction/addiction-health (accessed 2012).

Inhalants

Chemicals in common household products can get you "high," but often at a high cost to your health.

If you've ever come across a smelly marker, you've experienced an inhalant. They seem harmless, but they can actually be quite dangerous. Inhalants are chemical vapors that people inhale on purpose to get "high." The vapors produce mind-altering, and sometimes disastrous, effects. These vapors are in a variety of products common in almost any home or workplace. Examples are some paints, glues, gasoline, and cleaning fluids. Many people do not think of these products as drugs because they were never meant to be used to achieve an intoxicating effect. But when they are intentionally inhaled to produce a "high," they can cause serious harm.

Source: NIDA for Teens, "Facts on Drug Inhalants," http://teens.drugabuse.gov/drug-facts/inhalants.

Marijuana

Think everyone does it? And a bunch of leaves must be harmless, right? Check the facts.

Marijuana has a chemical in it called delta-9-tetrahydrocannabinol, better known as THC. A lot of other chemicals are found in marijuana, too—about four hundred of them, many of which could affect your health. But THC is the main psychoactive (i.e., mind altering) ingredient. In fact, marijuana's strength or potency is related to the amount of THC it contains. The THC content of marijuana has been increasing since the 1970s. For the year 2007, estimates from confiscated marijuana indicated that it contains almost 10 percent THC, on average.

Some research says that more kids go into drug treatment for marijuana than for all other combined illicit drugs. The part of the brain where memories are formed is affected by the active ingredient in marijuana. This drug can affect your body and brain. There is four times as much cancer-causing tar in a single joint than a filtered cigarette, and there are at least four hundred chemicals in marijuana. Other names: nail, roach, blunt, joint, Mary Jane, ganja, reefer, grass, pot, weed.

Source: NIDA, "Drugs, Brains, and Behavior: The Science of Addiction," www.drugabuse.gov/publications/science-addiction/addiction-health (accessed 2012).

Methamphetamine

Did you know that meth is a powerful, addictive drug that can cause permanent psychological damage? An overdose can kill you. If it doesn't kill you, it can cause damage to the brain; you may become paranoid or think in ways not true to reality. Meth causes damage to the body as well, perhaps giving you a stroke, not to mention high blood pressure. For those who inject with needles, you are at risk for HIV/AIDS. Other terms: black beauties, go fast, ice, glass, uppers, crank, tweak, crystal, meth, speed.

Source: NIDA, "Drugs, Brains, and Behavior: The Science of Addiction," www.drugabuse.gov/publications/science-addiction/addiction-health (accessed 2012).

Mixing Drugs and Alcohol

While any type of consumption of drugs or alcohol can be extremely dangerous, mixing them can lead to serious health issues and even death.

Source: NIDA, "Drugs, Brains, and Behavior: The Science of Addiction," www.drugabuse.gov/publications/science-addiction/addiction-health (accessed 2012).

Nicotine

What about nicotine? According to Arlene Hirschfelder in her book *Kick Butts*,

> Nicotine is a potent drug that occurs naturally in the leaves of Nicotiana tabacum. It is one of the most harmful poisons known. One drop of it in a concentrated state is enough to kill a dog. Eight drops of nicotine will kill a horse in four minutes. Nicotine does not kill the smoker because it is absorbed over a period of time. The body breaks it down and eliminates it in urine. Nicotine is absorbed by the body at remarkable speed. After a smoker inhales cigarette smoke into his or her lungs, nicotine transfers directly from the tiny airholes in the lungs into the bloodstream. From there, inhaled nicotine rushes to the brain in less than 10 seconds. It reaches the big toe in 14 to 20 seconds. It is also well absorbed through the very thin skin of the mouth or the nose which is dense with capillaries. That is why chewing tobacco and inhaling snuff are such effective ways to take in nicotine. Nicotine is an addictive drug. Some experts say it is the most addictive drug there is—more so than heroin or alcohol. It affects mood, feeling, and behavior by entering the brain and causing some effect.

Cigarettes are very addictive because of the nicotine they contain.

Here is something else to consider. When you smoke, you put the health and well-being of other people at risk. Breathing secondhand smoke raises their chances of getting lung cancer. Smoking is a lose-lose situation. Other names:

Cigarettes—smokes, butts, cigs. Smokeless tobacco—spit tobacco, snuff, chew, dip.

Sources: Arlene Hirschfelder, *Kick Butts: A Kid's Action Guide to a Tobacco-Free America* (Julian Messner, 1998); NIDA: "Drugs, Brains, and Behavior: The Science of Addiction," www.drugabuse.gov/publications/science-addiction/addiction-health (accessed 2012).

Prescription Drug Abuse and Party Drugs

Abusing prescription drugs is illegal and can be very dangerous.

There's a reason that prescription drugs are intended to be taken under the direction of a doctor: if used improperly they can be harmful. Teens are making the decision to abuse prescription medicines based on misinformation. In fact, many people think that abusing prescription drugs is safer than abusing illicit drugs. As the facts will tell you, prescription drugs can have short- and long-term health consequences when used incorrectly or by someone other than for whom they were intended.

Many teenagers have taken to ingesting over-the-counter and prescription medicines. These drugs have a specific use and can help people who are sick. But these are specifically prescribed for patients with certain symptoms or maladies. Teens taking these drugs are at risk for a number of dangers, such as addiction, withdrawal symptoms, and overdose, as well as damage to organs, change of attitude, high blood pressure, and more. Contrary to popular belief, getting high with prescription medications is not a safer way to get high.

An example is cough medicine abuse. This involves ingesting large doses of cough medicine to create a high, which can cause many harmful effects. The most commonly abused pain relievers are Vicodin, OxyContin, Ritalin, Adderall, Valium, and Xanax.

Source: NIDA, "Drugs, Brains, and Behavior: The Science of Addiction," www.drugabuse.gov/publications/science-addiction/addiction-health (accessed 2012).

Stimulants

This class of drugs can elevate mood and increase energy, but they are highly addictive.

Can these drugs be lethal? Yes, in rare instances, sudden death can occur on the first use of cocaine or unexpectedly thereafter. And, like most drugs, stimulants can be lethal when taken in large doses or mixed with other substances. Stimulant overdoses can lead to heart problems, strokes, hyperthermia (elevated body temperature), and convulsions, which if not treated immediately can result in death. Abuse of both cocaine and alcohol compounds the danger, increasing the risk of overdose. Street names for amphetamines include speed, bennies, black beauties, crosses, hearts, LA turnaround, truck drivers, and uppers.

Source: NIDA for Teens, "Facts on Drugs, Stimulants," http://teens.drug abuse.gov/drug-facts/stimulants.

Tobacco

Is nicotine the only harmful part of tobacco? No. Nicotine is only one of more than four thousand chemicals, many of which are poisonous, found in the smoke from tobacco products. Smokeless tobacco products also contain many toxins, as well as high levels of nicotine. Many of these other ingredients are things we would never consider putting in our bodies, like tar, carbon monoxide, acetalde-hyde, and nitrosamines. Tar causes lung cancer, emphysema, and bronchial diseases. Carbon monoxide causes heart problems, which is one reason why smokers are at high risk for heart disease.

Source: NIDA for Teens, "Facts on Drugs," http://teens.drugabuse.gov/facts/index.php (accessed January 2013).

Tobacco and Smoking

What is the most common cause of lung cancer? You've got it—smoking. Cancer of the mouth, throat, bladder, pancreas, and kidneys are caused most often by smoking. Smoking can also give you discolored teeth and also cause you to lose your teeth. For teens, when your body is still growing and changing, it can affect your normal development. Did you know that there are two hundred known poisons in cigarette smoke? Cigarette smoke can cause heart disease, bronchitis, and even strokes not to mention giving you dry skin, causing wrinkles, and maybe even causing hair loss and grey hair even if you aren't old yet. And it can do even more damage.

Source: NIDA for Teens, "Facts on Tobacco," http://teens.drugabuse.gov/drug-facts/tobacco.

Appendix B: Contributors

Adult Contributors

"Alisa," performer, children's musical director

Jori Azinger, L.Ac. (Licensed Acupuncturist), HeartSpace (www.myheart space.org/; jori@myheartspace.org)

Patricia Bittner, the methamphetamine community policing coordinator for the Leech Lake Tribal Police Department on the Leech Lake Reservation, Minnesota

Dr. Ryan R. Byrne, assistant professor at the Medical College of Wisconsin, child and adolescent psychiatrist at Children's Hospital of Wisconsin

"Carol," contributor

Paula DeStefanis Christensen, Paula's Palette (http://paulaspalette.me; Yvonne Wakim Dennis, author www.theartsmill.org/artists-/paula-christensen/)

Judith Ford, psychotherapist, LCSW, Wisconsin

Tom Frank, chief of police, Wisconsin

Karen Glassman, MSW, MBA, Wisconsin

Arlene Hirschfelder, author, editor

Janis Kinens, pastor

Donna Bestor Krieger, former coordinator of the Alliance for a Drug-Free Wisconsin established by Governor Tommy Thompson, Attorney General Don Hanaway, and State Superintendent of Schools Herbert Grover

Rick Leach, sergeant, Wisconsin

Karl A. Lickteig, DC, CCSP, CCEP, certified chiropractic sports and extremities practitioner team chiropractor, Milwaukee Buck's Organization; NBA Disability Consultant, Northwestern Mutual, Milwaukee

John R. Mabry, SAC-IT (substance abuse counselor in training)

Dr. Gabor Maté, author, public speaker

Janet Osherow, LICSW, family services coordinator, Maryland

Bonnie Raettig, mother of Angela

Dr. Norm Schwartz, integrated medicine

Barrie Springhetti, LMT, board director of Unified Body Wellness Institute

Pandit Rajmani Tigunait, PhD, spiritual head of the Himalayan Institute, author

Reverend Kenneth Wheeler, Wisconsin

Career Contributions

"Alex," CEO of three boys
Darya Alexander, MD/family physician
Jennifer Bergen, mom/photographer/writer
Helen Butler, reading intervention specialist
Sgt. Kip Butler, police sergeant
Tom Frank, chief of police officer
Paula Hare, creative director for Hare Strigenz Inc. and Paula Hare and Associates
Steve Heston, founder and managing principal, The Heston Group, LLC
"Jane," business consultant/manager
"John," ski lift operator
Jalil Keval, vice president of sales
Kathleen Koster, coordinator and box office manager for a performing arts center
Lt. Frederick Martin, U.S. Navy public affairs officer
Mike Nichols, writer
"Paul," appellate attorney
Sandy Williams, Ozaukee County Circuit Court judge
"WS," management consultant

Fact Checkers/Editing Help

Dr. Ryan R. Byrne, assistant professor at the Medical College of Wisconsin, child and adolescent psychiatrist at Children's Hospital of Wisconsin
John Mabry, SAC-IT
Mike Nichols, author

Teen Contributors

"Angela"—Bonnie (Angela's mom) shared writing of Angela's and memories of her story, which began in middle school.
"Arturo"—Shared memories of his story, which began in high school.
"Brady"—Shared memories of his story, which began in elementary school.
"Brian"—Shared memories of his story, which began as a junior in high school.
"Carol"—Shared memories of her story, which began in college.
"Jessica"—Shared memories of her story, which began in middle school.
"Kyle"—Shared memories of his story, which began in college.

"Lily"—Shared memories as an eighth grader.

"Lon"—Shared memories of his story, which began as a freshman in high school.

"Princess Peach"—Shared memories of her story, which began in middle school.

"Tim"—Shared memories of his story, which began in high school.

"Tristessa"—Shared memories of her story, which began in high school.

Teen Artists

Nikolas Abendroth
Hailie Bestor
Angela Raettig

Additional Teens, Who Shared Insights

Hailie Bestor
Kaiti Bestor
Whitnie Bestor

Appendix C:
Great Sources/Bibliography

Some reads on the topic of substance use and abuse can be found on page 115.

Websites and/or Pamphlets

Beliefnet. "Yoga for Teens." www.beliefnet.com/Wellness/Yoga/Teen-Yoga/ Yoga-for-Teens.aspx (accessed 2012).

CASAColumbia: The National Center on Addiction and Substance Abuse at Columbia University. www.casacolumbia.org/templates/Home.aspx?articleid =287 (accessed 2012).

Centers for Disease Control and Prevention. "National Vital Statistics Report," April 17, 2009. www.cdc.gov/nchs/data/nvsr/nvsr57/nvsr57_14.pdf (accessed November 19, 2012).

Esherick, Joan. *Dying for Acceptance: A Teen's Guide to Drug- and Alcohol-Related Health Issues.* Philadelphia: Mason Crest, 2005.

Girlshealth.gov. www.girlshealth.gov (accessed November 2012).

Healthy Parks, Healthy People Central. www.hphpcentral.com (accessed 2012).

HelpGuide.org. www.helpguide.org/about.htm (accessed November 2012).

Hyde, Margaret O., and John F. Setaro. *Drugs 101: An Overview for Teens.* Brookfield, CT: Twenty-First Century, 2003.

Joseph, George. "Social Media's Effect on Adolescents." www.rightstep.com/ blog/social-media-effects-on-adolescents.html (accessed 2012).

Kassem, Noreen. "Environmental Factors that Contribute to Drug Abuse." Livestrong.com. www.livestrong.com/article/250843-environmental-factors -that-contribute-to-drug-abuse (accessed 2012).

KidsHealth from Nemours.kidshealth.org (accessed November 2012).

Livestrong.org. www.livestrong.org (accessed November 2012).

Miller, William R. *Enhancing Motivation for Change in Substance Abuse Treatment.* Rockville, MD: U.S. Dept. of Health and Human Services, Public Health Service, Substance Abuse and Mental Health Services Administration, Center for Substance Abuse Treatment, 1999.

National Institute on Drug Abuse. www.drugabuse.gov (accessed 2012).

National Institute on Drug Abuse. "Director's Page." www.drugabuse.gov/about-nida/directors-page (accessed 2012).

"Some Brain Wiring Continues to Develop Well into Our 20s." *Science Daily*. http://www.sciencedaily.com/releases/2011/09/110922134617.htm.

Streetdrugs.org. streetdrugs.org (accessed 2012).

Substance Abuse and Mental Health Services Administration. www.samhsa.gov. (accessed 2012).

"Teen Drug Abuse Statistics: Top 5 Government Sites." *AddictionBlog.org* (blog), November 18, 2010. addictionblog.org/the-news/teen-drug-abuse-statistics -top-5-government-sites (accessed 2012).

"Youth Drug Use: The Good, the Bad, and the Ugly." *The White House.gov* (blog). January 11, 2012. www.whitehouse.gov/blog/2012/01/11/youth-drug -use-good-bad-and-ugly (accessed 2012).

Books

Carr, Kris. *Crazy Sexy Diet: Eat Your Veggies, Ignite Your Spark, and Live Like You Mean It!* Guilford, CT: Skirt!, 2011.

Diagnostic and Statistical Manual of Mental Disorders, Fourth Edition: Primary Care Version (DSM-IV-PC). Washington, DC: American Psychiatric Association, 1995.

Fletcher, Anne M. *Inside Rehab: The Surprising Truth about Addiction Treatment— and How to Get Help That Works*. New York: Viking for Adults, 2013.

Hanna, Thomas. *Somatics: Reawakening the Mind's Control of Movement, Flexibility, and Health*. Reading, MA: Addison-Wesley, 1988.

Hirschfelder, Arlene. *A Kid's Action Guide to a Tobacco-Free America: Kick Butts!* New York: Julian Messner, 1998.

Maté, Gabor. *In the Realm of Hungry Ghosts: Close Encounters with Addiction*. Berkeley, CA: North Atlantic, 2010.

Neufeld, Gordon, and Gabor Maté. *Hold on to Your Kids: Why Parents Need to Matter More Than Peers*. New York: Ballantine, 2006.

Rath, Tom, and Donald O. Clifton. *How Full Is Your Bucket?* New York: Gallup, 2010.

Rompella, Natalie. *Obsessive-Compulsive Disorder: The Ultimate Teen Guide*. Lanham, MD: Scarecrow, 2009.

Sahley, Billie Jay, Katherine M. Birkner, and Billie Jay Sahley. *Heal with Amino Acids and Nutrients: Survive Stress, Pain, Anxiety, Depression without Drugs: What to Use and When*. San Antonio, TX: Pain & Stress Publications, 2000.

Schneck, Daniel J., Dorita S. Berger, and Geoffrey Rowland. *The Music Effect: Music Physiology and Clinical Applications*. London: Jessica Kingsley, 2006.

Selhub, Eva M., and Alan C. Logan. *Your Brain on Nature: The Science of Nature's Influence on Your Health, Happiness and Vitality*. Mississauga, Ont.: John Wiley & Sons Canada, 2012.

Smolen, Jamie R. *Hooked*. Albuquerque, NM: Casa De Snapdragon Pub., 2011.

Stein, Michael. *The Addict: One Patient, One Doctor, One Year*. New York: Harper Perennial, 2010.

Resources Providing Holistic Programming

The following are a few holistic sources the author was connected with at the time this book was published. Please also refer to the contributors and the sources they are connected with.

Himalayan Institute. www.himalayaninstitute.org
Balancing Arts Yoga and Well Being Studio. www.balancingartsyoga.com
North Shore Academy of the Arts, Inc. www.northshoreacademyofthearts.org
Fon du Lac Center for Spirituality and Healing. www.fcsh.org

Treatment Centers or More Resources for Treatment

Behavior Health Treatment Services. http://findtreatment.samhsa.gov
Betty Ford Center. www.bettyfordcenter.org/index.php
Center for Substance Abuse Treatments. www.samhsa.gov/about/csat.aspx
The Treatment Center. www.thetreatmentcenter.com

Art

American Art Therapy Association (AATA). arttherapy.org. Describes the therapeutic process of art therapy.

Creative Arts Resources, Provided by the Addiction Recovery Guide. www.addictionrecoveryguide.org/holistic/creative_arts_therapy.

Creative Guide through the 12 Steps. creative12steps.com. This blog page offers instructions for using creative arts projects as a supplement to working the 12 steps.

National Coalition of Arts Therapies Associations. nccata.org

Dance

American Dance Therapy Association (ADTA). adta.org

Drama

National Association for Drama Therapy (NADT). nadt.org

Music

American Music Therapy Association (AMTA). musictherapy.org
Drumming. www.ncbi.nlm.nih.gov

Poetry

National Association for Poetry Therapy (NAPT). poetrytherapy.org

Appendix D: Teen Insights through Art on Substance Abuse

The contributors and I have shared ideas and thoughts about substance abuse through interviews and writings. This section of the book includes insights by teens through artwork.

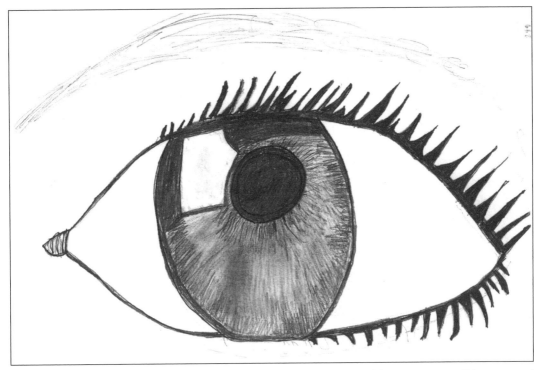

"My drawing is of an eye. It means that I feel teens need to be able to see everything around them, which includes seeing when someone is pressuring you. Can you see what I mean?"
—Hailie Bestor

By Nik Abendroth

"Most of my sketches were derived from the meaning or message behind the text. From underage drinking, to smoking and use of tobacco products, and even the emotions that are felt within those who are stuck in the addiction or cycle of various uses of alcohol to narcotics simply to ease the pain felt by some. My sketch with the teen girl balancing on the edge really emphasized the feeling of loneliness. Although the addiction is not healthy and not needed by any, to a regular user the lift is the only thing that's there when times are rough. Other sketches simply depict the different types of substance abuse, and mainly the places they fill in a teen's life that seem empty through the years of high school in general."—Nik Abendroth

By Angela Raettig

By Angela Raettig

By Angela Raettig

Index

About the Author

Sheri Mabry Bestor is a member of Society of Children's Books Writers and Illustrators and a published book author. She has worked as a freelance writer for local newspapers and magazines and has sold work locally and nationally to magazines. Sheri earned her BS in elementary education from the University of Wisconsin, Madison, and her MA in curriculum and instruction. She is an experienced elementary teacher, tennis instructor, drama instructor, and theater director. She is a yoga instructor certified by the Himalayan Teachers Association and a registered yoga instructor through Yoga Alliance. She is a guide for yoga and somatic movement methods, as well as a Reiki master.

Sheri is the founder and president of North Shore Academy of the Arts, Inc., a not-for-profit organization offering quality opportunities in the visual, performing, and literary arts. She is the owner of Balancing Arts, a yoga and well-being studio.

Sheri lives with her family in a small town in the Midwest. Her website is www.sheribestor.com.